FREEDOM TRAIN
NORTH

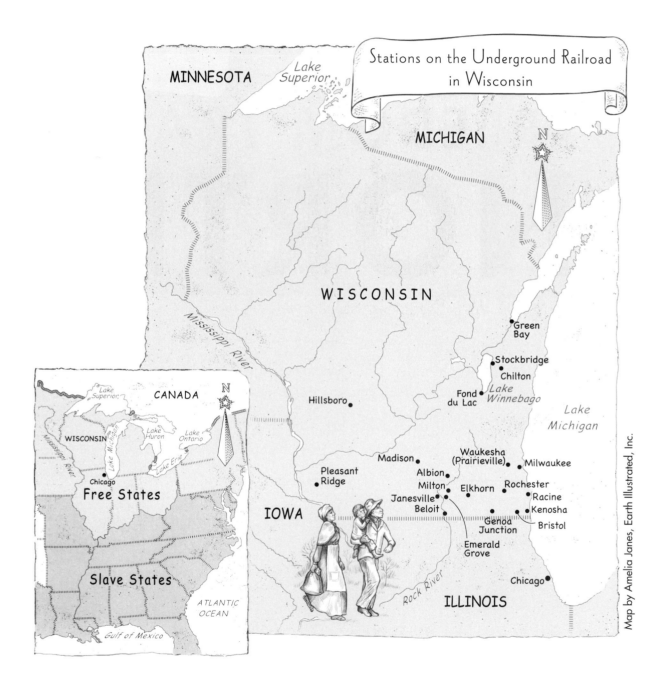

Stations on the Underground Railroad in Wisconsin

MINNESOTA

Lake Superior

MICHIGAN

N

WISCONSIN

Mississippi River

Green Bay
Stockbridge
Chilton
Fond du Lac
Lake Winnebago

Hillsboro

Lake Michigan

Madison
Waukesha (Prairieville)
Milwaukee
Albion
Milton
Elkhorn
Rochester
Pleasant Ridge
Janesville
Racine
Beloit
Genoa Junction
Kenosha
Bristol
Emerald Grove

IOWA

Rock River

Chicago

ILLINOIS

CANADA

Lake Superior

N

WISCONSIN

Lake Huron
Lake Ontario
Lake Erie

Mississippi River

Lake Michigan

Chicago

Free States

Slave States

ATLANTIC OCEAN

Gulf of Mexico

Map by Amelia Janes, Earth Illustrated, Inc.

FREEDOM TRAIN
NORTH

Stories of the Underground Railroad in Wisconsin

Julia Pferdehirt

WISCONSIN HISTORICAL SOCIETY PRESS

Published by the Wisconsin Historical Society Press
Publishers since 1855

© 2011 by the State Historical Society of Wisconsin

First edition published in 1998.
Wisconsin Historical Society Press edition 2011.

wisconsinhistory.org

Photographs identified with WHi or WHS are from the Society's collections; address requests to reproduce these photos to the Visual Materials Archivist at the Wisconsin Historical Society, 816 State Street, Madison, WI 53706.

Front cover images: reward poster, WHi Image ID 1926; fugitive slave, WHi Image ID 41426; compass, istockphoto.com; background map, WHi Image ID 77589;
Back cover image: tunnel, courtesy of the Milton Historical Society.

Printed in Wisconsin, U.S.A.
Designed by Mark Skowron Design, LLC

15 14 13 12 11   1 2 3 4 5

Library of Congress Cataloging-in-Publication Data
Pferdehirt, Julia, 1952-
Freedom train North : stories of the Underground Railroad in Wisconsin / Julia Pferdehirt.
     p. cm.—(Freedom train North)
Originally published: 1998.
Includes bibliographical references and index.
ISBN 978-0-87020-474-6 (pbk. : alk. paper) 1. Underground railroad—Wisconsin. 2. Fugitive slaves—Wisconsin—History—19th century. 3. Antislavery movements—Wisconsin—History—19th century. I.Title.
 E450.P535 2011
 973.7'115—dc22

                         2010050402

∞ The paper used in this publication meets the minimum requirements of the American National Standard for Information Sciences—Permanence of Paper for Printed Library Materials, ANSI Z39.48-1992.

To the many children in schools across the state of Wisconsin who have heard me tell stories of the Underground Railroad from our history. Enjoy these true stories!

CONTENTS

PREFACE

Between the covers of this book are stories of people with dreams of freedom. Each is a true story of the Underground Railroad. The people who lived these true stories were children and teenagers, women and men. Some owned big houses and others lived in tiny cabins they built with their own hands. There were college professors and ministers, teachers and farmers, immigrants, soldiers, and even steamboat captains. Blacks, whites, and American Indians joined together to become the Underground Railroad in Wisconsin.

When a story includes spoken words, those words were actually said or written by these people many years ago. Thoughts and feelings described were also recorded by the people who experienced them. However, when personal accounts were not recorded, you may be asked to imagine how people felt and thought.

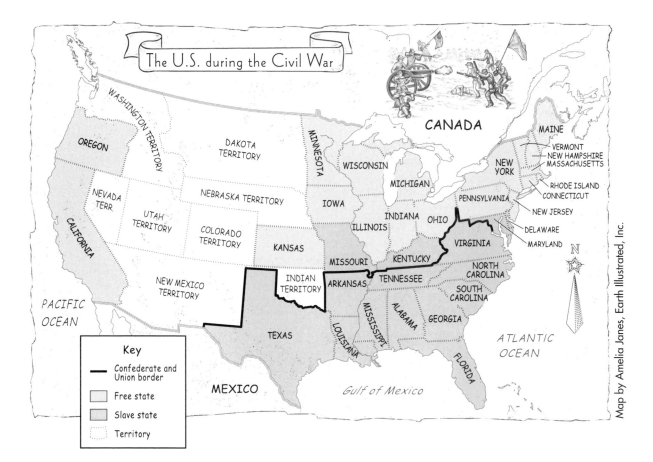

The U.S. during the Civil War

CANADA

WASHINGTON TERRITORY

OREGON

DAKOTA
TERRITORY

MINNESOTA

WISCONSIN

MAINE

VERMONT
NEW HAMPSHIRE
MASSACHUSETTS

NEVADA
TERR.

NEBRASKA TERRITORY

MICHIGAN

NEW
YORK

RHODE ISLAND
CONNECTICUT

CALIFORNIA

UTAH
TERRITORY

IOWA

PENNSYLVANIA

NEW JERSEY

COLORADO
TERRITORY

INDIANA

OHIO

DELAWARE

KANSAS

ILLINOIS

VIRGINIA

MARYLAND

MISSOURI

KENTUCKY

N

NEW MEXICO
TERRITORY

INDIAN
TERRITORY

ARKANSAS

TENNESSEE

NORTH
CAROLINA

PACIFIC
OCEAN

SOUTH
CAROLINA

ALABAMA

GEORGIA

ATLANTIC
OCEAN

TEXAS

LOUISIANA

MISSISSIPPI

FLORIDA

MEXICO

Gulf of Mexico

Key

— Confederate and
Union border

Free state

Slave state

Territory

Map by Amelia Janes, Earth Illustrated, Inc.

INTRODUCTION
History, Legend, and Story

Stories. Don't you love them? Remember Paul Bunyan fixing flapjacks for breakfast—greasing a griddle the size of a football field with slabs of bacon tied to his boots like ice skates?

Paul Bunyan tales, flapjacks and all, have been told and retold in Wisconsin. Although they might have begun long ago with a real lumberjack who cut faster, jumped higher, and lifted more than anyone else, everyone knows they are not true. They are legends.

What about history? History is told and retold too. Over the years, the stories change until no one knows *exactly* what happened. People wonder if 100 **fugitive** slaves really boarded steamships in Racine. Maybe it was 500. Or more. Did 1,000 people really smash the jail door with a battering ram to free Joshua Glover in Milwaukee? How do we know?

---

fugitive (**fyoo** juh tiv): someone who is running away, especially from the police

True stories, like those in this book, are *history*. Historians have the exciting but challenging job of deciding what is history and what is not. Underground Railroad history is especially challenging because the secrecy needed to protect freedom workers and fugitive slaves meant that very little was **documented** in writing.

Courtesy of the Ohio Historical Society

A. P. Dutton was a freedom worker in Racine.

All stories in this book were well documented. Some were recorded in books and newspapers. For example, newspapers reported Joshua Glover's rescue. Some stories were saved in diaries or books called **memoirs**—collections of memories. From an army **chaplain**'s memoirs we know **Colonel** William Utley shouted, "Fix bayonets!" as the 22nd Wisconsin Volunteer **Regiment** marched through Louisville using their guns to protect fugitive slaves in the center of the regiment.

History is sometimes recorded in letters. Historians know at least 100 fugitive slaves escaped from Racine because A. P. Dutton wrote about it in a letter.

---

documented: recorded with factual support
memoir (**mem** wahr): a true story written about a person's own life
chaplain: a priest, minister, or rabbi who works in the military
colonel (**kur** nuhl): an officer in the U.S. Army, Air Force, or Marine Corps ranking below a general
regiment: a military unit made up of 500 to 1,000 soldiers

In 1880 Caroline Quarlls wrote to her friend Lyman Goodnow. Two letters, along with a third from Caroline's husband telling the story of his own escape from slavery, were tucked inside a box and forgotten. Then in 1998, more than 100 years later, Lyman Goodnow's descendants in Waukesha, Wisconsin, found them. Reading those letters is like meeting Caroline face-to-face. Her words reach across 150 years of history to today.

The past is also told through **oral history**. Unlike Paul Bunyan tales, which everyone knows are invented, oral history is *told*. Sometimes stories are passed from one person to another. Both teller and listener know the stories told through oral history are important to pass down to the next **generation**.

Sometimes, these told stories are recorded. The storyteller remembers the words, and an interviewer writes them down. Sometimes these memories are **accurate**. Sometimes so much time has passed that the memories become **distorted**. Facts might be lost or details might change over time. The oral historian just needs to find other **evidence** to make sure that the details remembered in the stories are correct.

African storytellers called *griots* were, and still are, honored as keepers of history. When slaves in the United States were not allowed to read or write, the practice of saving the past through oral history continued.

---

oral history: history that is spoken, not written
generation: all the people born around the same time
accurate: exactly correct
distorted: changed or twisted
evidence: information and facts that help prove something is true
griot (**gree** oh)

Newspapers like *Freedom's Journal* give us clues to what happened in the fight to end slavery in America.

Stories are told and retold. Sometimes bits are forgotten, or details change, but the heart of the story remains. The story in this book of Theodore Fellows bringing a fugitive slave to Kellogg's Tavern was *told* for many years before it was written down.

Members of one Wisconsin family kept its history alive by telling and retelling a story about their **ancestor** Samuel Arms and his **Civil War** drum. This is the story:

Toward the end of the Civil War, 12-year-old Samuel Arms was a slave in Georgia. One day his master's daughter hit him with a riding whip. He grabbed it. In the struggle Samuel struck the woman. What had he done? For a slave to touch a white woman was unthinkable. His master would kill him. Samuel ran away to save his own life.

---

ancestor: member of a family who lived a long time ago
Civil War: the U.S. war between the southern states, or Confederacy, and the northern states, or Union, that lasted from 1861 to 1865

At that time, war had turned Georgia into a battlefield. The land looked as if a giant hand had swept across it, crushing and uprooting everything. Soldiers died by the thousands. **Refugees** wandered hungry and homeless. One of those refugees was Samuel Arms.

Samuel was alone. Perhaps hunger brought him to the camp of a Union regiment from Pennsylvania. Perhaps he hoped the soldiers would protect him from his master. No one knows. But, as the Arms family remembers, an officer hired Samuel as a servant.

Samuel was bright and good with horses. He became the regiment's drummer and followed his employer to Pennsylvania after the war. Samuel took his drum with him. Years later, he set out for the **prairies** and hills of western Wisconsin to work as a horse trainer in the pioneer town of Hillsboro.

Samuel Arms married Mary Roberts. They filled their small house with at least 12 children. Samuel told them how he escaped from slavery and had once been a drummer in President Lincoln's army. For many years he marched in the **annual veterans'** parades. He always set the pace to march with a steady beat on his drum.

WHi Image ID 45965

Samuel Arms and his family at their home in Wisconsin

---

refugee: someone who is forced to leave his or her home because of war, persecution, or natural disaster
prairie: a large area of flat or rolling grassland with few or no trees
annual: happening once every year
veteran: someone who has served in the armed forces

Today, Samuel Arms's story and his drum belong to his grandchildren, great-grandchildren, and great-great-grandchildren. The drum is a symbol of his life. It is a symbol, too, of his family's history and of African American people fighting for their freedom. The Arms family shared this history with all Wisconsin by lending the drum for **exhibit** at the Wisconsin Historical Museum in Madison.

Samuel Arms's story is not the only Wisconsin story about slavery, slaves, and freedom. Tales about the Underground Railroad are told all over the state—perhaps even in your community. Some are history. Some are legends.

How do historians know which stories are true and which are legends? They become detectives. They examine stories as a crime investigator examines clues. Historians ask questions, hunt for information, and fit clues together like a thousand-piece jigsaw puzzle.

Suppose someone said a house in your town was once an Underground Railroad station. How would you find out if that was true?

First, you might look for documents like old newspapers, books, letters, or diaries. Historical societies, libraries, churches, and families that have lived in your community since the 1800s are good sources. Your librarian can help.

Next, ask questions. Were accounts written by eyewitnesses? How old is the information? Did your town have an **antislavery** society? Are known Underground Railroad stations nearby?

---

exhibit: a display at a museum
antislavery: against slavery

Then, interview community elders and people whose families have lived in Wisconsin since the 1850s. Prepare for interviews by scheduling a date and time. Tell the person you will be asking about Underground Railroad stories. Bring a list of questions and an audio recorder.

When your detective work is done, put the clues together. If you're lucky enough to find documents from the 1850s or 1860s mentioning fugitive slaves, you'll know your town's story is probably true.

Suppose you find your town is 10 miles from a known Underground Railroad station, and the old house in the story was owned by an antislavery society member. With this information, you can decide the story *might* be true.

If you just discover that an antislavery society met in the house, you do not have enough information. Sometimes historians just don't know if a story is true.

Finally, if you don't find any evidence, you can be almost certain the story is a legend and your town was not an Underground Railroad station.

This book tells almost all that is known today about the Underground Railroad in Wisconsin. No doubt more stories are waiting to be found. The people who find them must be willing to dig like **archaeologists**, think like detectives, and dream like storytellers. You can join the search for this important history. Just follow the tracks of Wisconsin's Underground Railroad.

---

archaeologist (ar kee **ol** uh jist): a scientist who learns about past people by studying objects left behind at places where people lived, worked, and played

William Hall's Journey

CANADA

N

MINNESOTA
TERRITORY

Lake Superior

Straits of Mackinac

Lake Michigan

WISCONSIN

Lake Huron

MICHIGAN

Detroit River

Milwaukee
Racine
Kenosha
Chicago

Lake Erie

IOWA

Free States

Bloomington

Springfield

INDIANA

OHIO

ILLINOIS

VIRGINIA

KENTUCKY

MISSOURI

Mississippi River

TENNESSEE

Slave States

ARKANSAS

ALABAMA

MISSISSIPPI

Map by Amelia Janes, Earth Illustrated, Inc.

1

FREEDOM DREAMS

"The overseer tied me to a tree and flogged me with the whip. . . . While he was eating supper, I got off my shoe, and slipped off a chain and ran."

William Hall had known only slavery from the day he was born until the day that overseer lifted his whip. But that day—that moment—William Hall said, *No more*. He ran for his life. Past dogs and through cold nights, he ran. Sometimes lost and always hungry, he ran. He begged for food, slept in the open, and kept running.

He ran north from Tennessee—when he could find north, that is. Sneaking in the dark through woods and crawling through cornfields turned him in circles. More than once he walked for days in the wrong direction. Where did he find the strength to walk those long miles back again? One night, cold rain wet him to the skin. The next night he hid in a barn, shivering with fever. Shaking, half-starved, and falling-down sick, William Hall made himself go on. Every step was one step closer to freedom.

He reached Illinois. "I got thirty miles out of my way again: so that when I reached Bloomington, I was too tired to go another step," he said. "I found an **abolitionist** who helped me to Chicago. From about the middle of August to the middle of November, I dwelt in no house except in Springfield. Sick. Had no bed till I got to Bloomington. In February, I cut wood in Indiana. I went to Wisconsin and staid [stayed] till harvest was over; then came to a particular friend."

"Now," his friend said, "square up your business, and go to the lake, for there are men here now, even here where you are living, who would **betray** you for half a dollar if they knew where your master is. Cross the lake! Get into Canada!"

William Hall's "particular friend" set him on the last miles of his long run to freedom. This friend, along with thousands of people like him, called himself an abolitionist. Abolitionists worked for the end of slavery. Some spoke out quietly. Some gave speeches or helped slaves run from their so-called masters.

A common symbol used by abolitionists

"Cross the lake! Get into Canada!" said William Hall's abolitionist friend. He sent Hall to the shore of Lake Michigan, where steamships set out on the long trip from Kenosha, Racine, or Milwaukee, north through the Straits of Mackinac, to Lake

---

abolitionist (ab uh **lish** uh nist): a person who is against slavery
betray: turn against someone, especially in a time of need

Huron's Canadian shore. A few ship captains were secret freedom workers. They were abolitionists who would **smuggle** any runaway north to Canada. In Canada, slavery was outlawed, and black people were free. It was there in 1856 that William Hall told his story. He was a free man at last.

The Underground Railroad started long before William Hall's time. It wasn't a railroad at all. There were no steam engines or tracks from one town to the next. What historians call the Underground Railroad was just people—freedom workers scattered all over North America who helped other people escape from slavery.

In some places, freedom workers organized schedules and stops like a real railroad. In other places, like Wisconsin, a few known and trusted friends worked together to help fugitive slaves.

As time passed, the Underground Railroad grew. Codes were sometimes used to keep their work secret. A safe house was sometimes called a "station." Workers were "conductors." An escaping person might be called "cargo" or a "parcel," another word for package. If a message came saying, "Three parcels due Tuesday," freedom workers expected 3 people in need of help and hope.

Workers on the Underground Railroad in Wisconsin were just like the people in your town. They were old and young, rich and poor, black, white, and American Indian. They were **pastors**, farmers, shopkeepers, steamboat captains, and homemakers. Their "stations" were barns and cabins, a tunnel, and once, even an empty sugar barrel!

---

smuggle: bring goods or people into a place illegally
pastor: a minister or priest in charge of a church

WHi Image ID 53060

The Detroit River in 1855. Many runaway slaves found freedom once they crossed this river and arrived in Canada.

Fugitive slaves took their freedom into their own hands. They said, *No more.* No more whips and chains. No more masters. No more seeing human beings bought and sold.

Because slavery was legal in the South and illegal in the northern states, most enslaved people ran north. Hungry, cold, and tired to the bone, they were chased by **bounty hunters** and **bloodhounds**. The road to freedom was hard. People hid in swamps, waded streams, and swam rivers. By day and in the middle of the night, over city streets and across wide, lonely prairies, they ran. Some ran alone. Others were helped by the Underground Railroad.

bounty hunter: a person who caught runaway slaves for money
bloodhound: a large dog with a wrinkled face, drooping ears, and a very good sense of smell

In 1850, the Fugitive Slave Law was passed. This law allowed slave catchers to capture runaways in any state. Slave catchers could go to free states like Wisconsin and drag people back to slavery. The law also punished anyone who helped people fleeing slavery.

Once the Fugitive Slave Law was passed, the only hope for freedom was to leave the United States, so people followed their freedom dreams to Canada. In Canada, slavery was outlawed, slave catchers were put in prison, and black people were free citizens.

Thousands of men, women, and children fled through Michigan and crossed the Detroit River. Others walked mile after mile through New York or Ohio. Still others followed the great Mississippi River or the shore of Lake Michigan. For some of them, the road to freedom passed through the new, wide-open land of Wisconsin. This is their story.

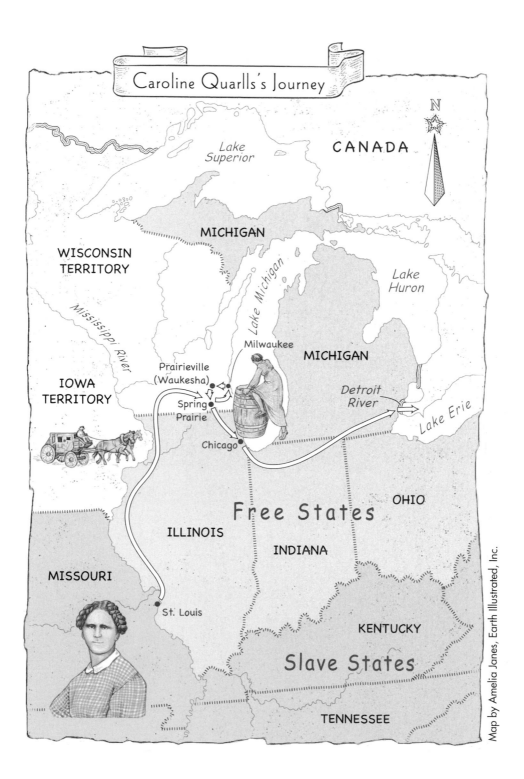

Caroline Quarlls's Journey

N

Lake Superior

CANADA

MICHIGAN

WISCONSIN TERRITORY

Lake Michigan

Lake Huron

IOWA TERRITORY

Mississippi River

Milwaukee

MICHIGAN

Prairieville (Waukesha)

Spring Prairie

Detroit River

Lake Erie

Chicago

Free States

OHIO

ILLINOIS

INDIANA

MISSOURI

St. Louis

KENTUCKY

Slave States

TENNESSEE

Map by Amelia Janes, Earth Illustrated, Inc.

2

INDEPENDENCE DAY

On July 4, 1842, while all St. Louis, Missouri, celebrated with picnics and parades, 16-year-old Caroline Quarlls declared her own Independence Day. She took $100 and a box of clothes and ran for the Mississippi River and for her freedom.

Caroline Quarlls

Caroline darted along side roads and down alleys to downtown St. Louis. Her running feet beat a rhythm on the wooden sidewalks. She dodged horses and people to reach the Mississippi River docks. There, as she slipped into the crowd of riverboat passengers, Caroline's light skin and brown hair were her only **disguises**. Would people think she was a white girl on an afternoon outing? She could only hope.

---

disguise: something that hides a person's identity

In 1842 the Mississippi River was like a highway with riverboats headed north and south. A few dollars for a ticket allowed Caroline to cross the river to the free state of Illinois. There she boarded a stagecoach and rode to the end of the line, 400 miles from her master, Charles Hall. The coach bumped and swayed and shook its way north to the Wisconsin **Territory** and the city of Milwaukee.

A steamboat on the Mississippi River

Milwaukee was new and rough compared to St. Louis. Wooden sidewalks stretched in front of brick and wooden buildings, and the streets smelled of people, horses, and taverns.

Caroline rode in a stagecoach like the one pictured here.

But in St. Louis, Caroline was a slave. She was property—just like Master Hall's high-stepping horses. In Wisconsin she was free. Caroline stepped from the stagecoach into another world and another life.

---

territory: a part of the U.S. not yet admitted as a state

A barber in Milwaukee's tiny community of free blacks and former slaves offered Caroline a place to stay until she found a job. Caroline and hard work were old friends. In slavery she had done everything from fancy lacework to scrubbing floors.

Then, reward posters appeared.

RUNAWAY SLAVE!
CAROLINE QUARLLS, AGE 16
$300 REWARD

Three hundred dollars! Caroline's barber friend saw the posters. He had once been a slave. He wouldn't betray Caroline, would he? Still, that reward was like a magnet. Three hundred dollars was a year's pay. He'd be rich. In the end, the barber traded his self-respect for that $300 by telling slave catchers where Caroline was hidden. Like hounds after a fox, they rushed to Milwaukee to find her.

The slave catchers were quick and clever. They planned to snatch Caroline and run. Couldn't someone stop them? Surely Milwaukee's abolitionists would not let a young girl be returned to slavery. Someone would raise a fist and shout, *Stop! Kidnappers!*

But it would be too late. The slave catchers' plan was intended to work so quickly that by the time the freedom-loving people heard the news, Caroline would be gone. She'd be back scrubbing floors in Master Hall's fine house, and the slave catchers would be counting reward money.

The plan would have been as smooth as ice on a pond but for one young abolitionist, **Asahel** Finch. By accident, Finch heard about a runaway slave staying in a barber's shack near the river. He heard the name Caroline Quarlls. He heard about slave catchers from St. Louis and knew someone must stop them. Mr. Finch realized *he* had to be that someone. There was no time to waste.

Armed with nothing but courage, the young freedom worker dashed to the barber's house. The slave catchers could show up at any minute. He had to convince Caroline to run; somehow he had to make her believe she'd been betrayed.

What did he say? Why did she trust him? No one knows. But he did convince her—and not a second too soon. Caroline bundled up her few possessions and followed Finch toward the river just minutes before the barber returned, bringing the slave catchers with him.

The slave catchers searched the barber's house. Empty! Where was that girl? Fighting mad, they threw the barber to the ground and beat him. Then, the hunt began. House by house they searched, pounding on doors, yelling, and demanding to know where Caroline was hidden.

Asahel (**a** suh hel)

WHi Image ID 6554

This is how Milwaukee looked around the time Caroline was there.

While the slave catchers searched, Caroline and Finch crawled along behind brush and weeds. Loud, angry shouts filled the air. How long before they were discovered?

Caroline and Finch decided she must hide. But where? The neighborhood was poor, with houses no bigger than chicken coops. No cellars or attics. They looked **desperately** for a hiding place while the slave catchers' voices grew louder and closer.

Suddenly, they spied an old wooden sugar barrel half-hidden by weeds. The barrel belonged to a black man. Could they use it? Could the man be trusted? With the slave catchers closing in, they had to take a chance.

---

desperately (**des** puh ruht lee): in immediate need of help

Mr. Finch pried the lid from the barrel and stuffed Caroline inside, petticoats and all! She could hardly move. Bang! He pounded the lid back on. Then he ran for help, leaving Caroline behind, alone.

Hour after hour on that sizzling August day, Caroline huddled inside the barrel. Imagine her cramping muscles and the smell of sweat and heat and old wood. How long could she stay squeezed inside a barrel? Every minute must have crawled by. What could she do? If Mr. Finch didn't come for her, the slave catchers would.

Past midnight, Caroline heard footsteps and voices. Someone was coming! She could not see. Imagine hearing the screech of rusty nails as the barrel was pried open and hoping, *hoping* the people outside were friends. Imagine the barrel's lid lifting. Had Mr. Finch brought help, or were slave catchers waiting?

It was Mr. Finch! His face must have been as welcome as water in a desert. Caroline was safe—for the moment, at least.

There, in the middle of the night on that Milwaukee street, Caroline Quarlls's journey on the Underground Railroad began. She hid first at the Browns' farm just outside Milwaukee. Then abolitionists took her 30 miles away near Prairieville (now called Waukesha) to Samuel and Lucinda **Daugherty**'s house.

For 3 weeks Caroline hid with the Daughertys. The slave catchers set up headquarters at Jones's Tavern in Prairieville and continued searching. They rode from town to town, bullying, threatening, and bribing. Hired spies watched every crossroad and bridge between Prairieville and Milwaukee. Meanwhile, freedom workers waited. Silence and secrecy were their best weapons.

Daugherty (**doh** uhr tee)

With a $300 reward posted, it seemed like half the county tried to find Caroline Quarlls, and the other half tried to keep her free. Years later, people remembered bounty hunters searching the whole countryside, "armed with pistols, whiskey, and warrants."

The slave catchers tried every trick. They spread lies, saying Caroline wanted to go home, but the abolitionists wouldn't let her. We just want to help a poor girl, they claimed. The slave catchers promised to give her freedom papers. They promised, but few people believed them.

Weeks passed. Caroline stayed hidden, but each day the slave catchers got closer. Then, late one afternoon, they stomped right up onto Samuel and Lucinda Daugherty's front porch! Caroline dashed to the cellar.

The only way out was a potato chute, a narrow, slippery opening from the cellar to the outdoors. She had come too far to give up! Caroline squeezed up the chute, pushing, pulling, and scrambling to the outside. Then, dragging her long skirts through the dirt, she crawled between rows of corn to the far end of a field and hid. Although the slave catchers searched until dark, they did not find her. Still, Caroline and her abolitionist friends knew she could not hide in cornfields forever. Something must be done.

The answer was clear: Caroline must go to Canada. But the question was *how.* Usually fugitive slaves escaped by ship, but bounty hunters hoping for that $300 reward swarmed like flies around every dock from Kenosha to Milwaukee.

Fortunately, 2 freedom workers, Deacon Ezra Mendall and Lyman Goodnow, volunteered to smuggle Caroline out of Prairieville. Ezra Mendall wasn't afraid of anything or anyone. As a young man, he had brawled and gambled and fought barehanded. In 1842 he was 60 years old and a church deacon, but even that hadn't settled him down. When slave catchers came to his farm looking for Caroline, he ran them off at gunpoint.

Lyman Goodnow as an older man

Lyman Goodnow was a man who finished what he started. He hated slavery and had no wife or children depending on him. So one night, with a borrowed horse and wagon, the 2 men stowed Caroline under straw in the back of the wagon and left Prairieville. Where were they headed? "Someplace safe" was all they knew.

All night the wagon bumped and jostled along the roads to Spring Prairie. Two brothers agreed to hide Caroline until Lyman Goodnow returned for her. Caroline was afraid. More strangers. More white faces. She looked at Mr. Goodnow with worry in her eyes. "Am I among friends?" she asked.

Driving back, Mr. Goodnow felt something under the seat. He reached down to find the biggest, sharpest pig-sticking knife he had ever seen. "Deacon, what is *this*?" he yelled.

"Oh, just something I brought along to pick my teeth with," said the deacon with a sly smile. If slave catchers had tried to take Caroline, Ezra Mendall was prepared to fight.

Back in Prairieville, worries and plans filled the next days to the brim. Years later Lyman Goodnow wrote, "The more we talked, the more fearful we were she would be found. Finally, we decided that one of us should go and take the girl through to some station on the Underground Railroad. They pitched upon me, being an old bachelor with no family[,] to do the job."

Goodnow wrote, "I rode to Deacon Edmund Clinton's and said I wanted his saddle, **bridle**, and all the money he had. I told him, 'I am going on a skeerup [possibly a "**scare-up**"], and I may be **obliged** to pay the Queen a visit before I get back. . . .' He handed me five dollars, all the money he had by him. That made eight dollars."

The "skeerup" to "pay the Queen a visit" was Goodnow's way of saying that he planned to make a trip to Canada, which Queen Victoria of England ruled. With $8 and a borrowed horse, Lyman Goodnow returned to Spring Prairie for Caroline. Freedom workers offered help and money. One man loaned his horse, and another gave a wagon and a harness.

That night, with $20, a pillowcase filled with food, and a letter asking for help from any abolitionist, Goodnow started for Canada, which was 500 miles away. He had Caroline with him, buried under hay and a buffalo robe in the back of the wagon. They drove south to Illinois, around Chicago, through Indiana, and up into Michigan.

---

bridle: straps that fit around a horse's head and mouth and are used to control it
scare-up: a trip to get something or finish something that is hard to do
obliged: expected to do something

Goodnow and Caroline hid by day and traveled at night. They stayed in **claim shanties**, grand houses, and **Quaker** settlements. Sometimes, rain drenched them. Black, moonless nights and twisting roads confused them. They were often hungry and exhausted. And they were always on the lookout for slave catchers.

They followed the Underground Railroad from station to station until they reached the Detroit River in Michigan. Even there, reward posters for Caroline had been posted, and a slave catcher from St. Louis prowled the docks. Freedom workers hired a ferryboat to cross the river.

When Caroline finally stepped off that boat, she cried with joy. Canada! Freedom! She could come and go, think and feel, dream and choose her own way. Since that Independence Day in St. Louis, Caroline Quarlls had traveled more than 1,000 miles on the Underground Railroad, from July until October of 1842. She had run from slave catchers, crouched in a sugar barrel, and crawled through a cornfield. She had slept on dirt floors, in feather beds, and buried under hay. At last, at long last, she had reached Canada. For the first time in her life, she was free.

Caroline Quarlls stayed in Canada. She learned to read and write. Then she married a **widower** named Allen Watkins. They had 6 children. Her new life was hard, but freedom was **precious**.

---

claim shanty: a rough hut or cabin, built to claim a piece of land
Quaker: a member of the Society of Friends, a Christian group that opposes war and prefers simple religious services
widower: a man whose wife has died
precious (**presh** uhs): very special or dear

In 1880, she wrote to her dear friend Lyman Goodnow. The beginning of that letter reads as follows:

Sandwich, April 17th

Dearest friend: pen and ink could hardly express my joy when I heard from you once more.

I am living and have to work very hard; but I have never forgotten you nor your kindness. I am still in Sandwich—the same place where you left me. Just as soon as the postmaster read the name to me—your name—my heart filled with joy and gladness. . . . Dearest friend, you don't know how rejoiced I feel since I heard from you. Answer this as soon as you get it and let me know how you are, and your address.

Original letter from Caroline to Lyman Goodnow

Courtesy of the Civil War Museum, Kenosha, Wisconsin

3

STRONG AGAINST SLAVERY

Imagine. Late at night, you're reading by the kerosene lamp while a snowstorm blows and wails outside. You hear a knock at the door. Who could it be? With the next farm 3 miles away, folks don't come calling in the middle of the night. Someone must be in trouble.

"Open up," a voice whispers. "Hurry!"

You put down your book and pull the door latch. Two men rush inside, stomping snow from their feet and slamming the door behind them. Thick woolen scarves hide their faces.

The taller man pulls his scarf away. It's Dr. Strong from Beloit! What is he doing out in this storm?

The second man turns to warm his hands at the potbellied stove. "I'm here to ask for your help. I know you can be trusted," says Dr. Strong. "Let me introduce you to Mr. Isaac James."

Mr. James turns from the stove. One look at his face tells you why Dr. Strong is out in a snowstorm in the middle of the night. Isaac James's skin is smooth and dark. Rich, deep brown. His eyes look tired and afraid. A runaway slave has come to your door.

"We need help," Dr. Strong says. "Captain Kilsey's ship, the *Chesapeake*, docks in Racine come Monday. Kilsey will take Isaac to Canada. Will you hide Isaac and take him to meet the *Chesapeake*?"

WHi Image ID 25822

It was safer for freedom workers to use a back road like this one when transporting a fugitive slave.

You have always spoken against slavery. Now you have the chance to stand behind your words. Will you? Of course. But *can* you? You sort through your mind for hiding places and back-road routes to Racine and realize you can't do this alone. You wonder. Who will help? Who can be trusted?

This story is imaginary. Only Dr. Strong and Captain Kilsey of the *Chesapeake* are real. But between 1840 and 1862, in big cities, tiny towns, and prairie cabins, Wisconsin freedom workers did ask, Who will help? Who can be trusted?

Freedom Train North

They trusted close friends or family members, someone at church, or an abolitionist neighbor. One by one, names were added to the small list of Wisconsin freedom workers. A network grew that became part of the Underground Railroad. In time, people running from slavery could travel from town to town to Lake Michigan.

Prairieville, now called Waukesha, gives us a good picture of Wisconsin's Underground Railroad. Most Prairieville freedom workers belonged to the First Congregational Church. Remember when Lyman Goodnow needed a horse? He didn't go to a stranger; he asked his brother-in-law. Samuel and Lucinda Daugherty hid Caroline Quarlls in their house. Down in Wauwatosa, their daughter and her preacher husband helped fugitive slaves too. And so the network grew.

Were all Wisconsin people abolitionists? No. William Hall's "particular friend" warned him about people who would "betray you for half a dollar." Even in freedom-loving Prairieville, the Daughertys' neighbor tried to turn Caroline over to slave catchers.

Feelings about slavery were strong in Wisconsin. Abolitionist newspapers were published in Racine, Prairieville, and Milwaukee. Sherman Booth, editor of the *Wisconsin Freeman*, spent a year in jail for helping a runaway slave.

Arguments about slavery exploded like dynamite. In newspaper columns, on street corners, and in the state **legislature**, people argued for or against slavery. This is the South's problem, not ours, some people thought. Others thought, If one person isn't free, then no one is truly free.

---

legislature (**lej** uh slay chur): an elected group of people who have the power to make or change laws for a city, state, or nation

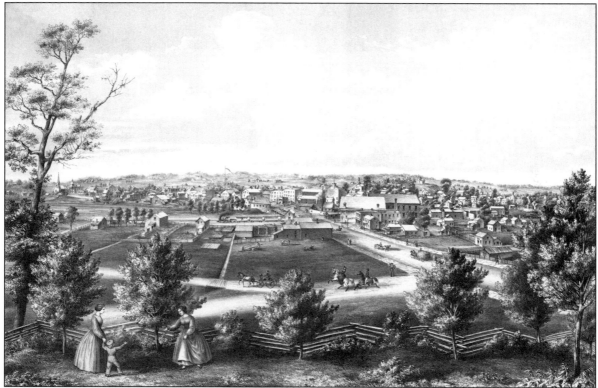

Prairieville (Waukesha) in 1857. Many people in Prairieville served as conductors on the Underground Railroad.

Some people fought slavery. Edward Mathews was a Baptist **missionary** who preached for God and against slavery all over Wisconsin for 20 years. When his missionary society accepted donations from southern slave owners, Mathews was furious. He refused his pay, saying he would never take a penny of slavers' money.

---

missionary (**mish** shuh nair ee): someone who is sent by a church or religious group to teach a group's faith

This poster advertises an abolitionist convention in Milwaukee in 1854.

Other people were **proslavery**. They ridiculed abolitionists and threw antislavery preachers like Mathews out of their churches.

Still other people were **fair-weather** abolitionists. In 1842, James Mitchell, chaplain to the Wisconsin legislature, said he was against slavery. But he actually kept 2 women as slaves. Abolitionists were shocked. He was breaking the law! Set them free, or lose your job, they said. **Reverend** Mitchell knew slavery was outlawed in Wisconsin, but he wanted to keep his slaves *and* his job. He boldly told everyone he didn't own a single slave. In fact, the slaves actually belonged to his wife! Finally, Mitchell secretly sent the 2 women to Virginia.

Wisconsin's freedom workers weren't many in number, but they stood strongly against slavery. Fifteen years after slavery ended, Lyman Goodnow wrote about his own town of Prairieville. "We were very **radical** in our views of right and wrong," he wrote. "We opposed bad men everywhere; supported all fugitive slaves who came to us, and worked like beavers for the right." These proud words could have been said about every freedom worker in Wisconsin.

Lyman Goodnow was correct; Wisconsin abolitionists *were* radical. Once, those radical freedom workers even became freedom *fighters*. That true story involves a fugitive slave, a battering ram, a jailbreak, and 1,000 angry abolitionists. It all began in faraway Missouri with a man named Joshua Glover.

---

proslavery: in favor of slavery
fair-weather: loyal only during a time of success
reverend: title used for a minister or other clergy
radical (**ra** di kuhl): extreme

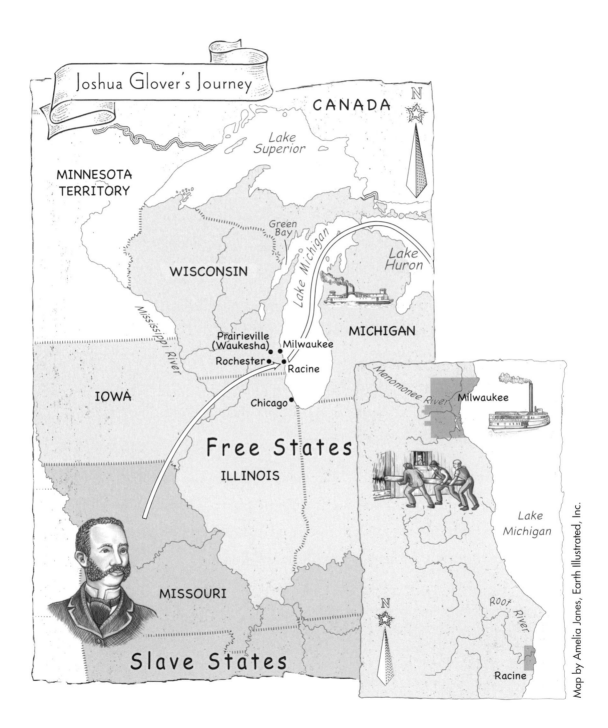

Joshua Glover's Journey

CANADA

N

Lake Superior

MINNESOTA
TERRITORY

Green Bay

Lake Michigan

Lake Huron

WISCONSIN

MICHIGAN

Prairieville
(Waukesha)
Rochester

Milwaukee

Racine

Mississippi River

IOWA

Chicago

Free States

ILLINOIS

MISSOURI

Slave States

Menomonee River

Milwaukee

Lake Michigan

N

Root River

Racine

Map by Amelia Janes, Earth Illustrated, Inc.

4

JAILBREAK!

In 1854, an antislavery storm rolled across Wisconsin. Newsboys on street corners **hawked** Sherman Booth's abolitionist paper, the *Wisconsin Freeman*, and steamship captains smuggled runaway slaves from Lake Michigan ports to Canada. Then, one spring night, slave catchers crept over the state line, and the people of Milwaukee and Racine had to take a stand for freedom.

In Missouri around 1851, a man named Joshua Glover had decided to "steal himself" from his master, Benami Garland. He ran and kept running until he reached Racine, Wisconsin, hundreds of miles away. In Racine, Glover found a job at the Rice and Sinclair Mill. He worked hard, saving money for land and a house. As he settled along the Root River, Joshua Glover did more than buy himself a home. He was building a whole new life.

By 1854, nearly 3 years later, Glover was settled and happy. One Saturday evening, he sat laughing and playing cards with 3 friends when, suddenly, someone pounded on the door. Open in the name of the law! It was U.S. Marshal Charles Cotton with a warrant for Joshua Glover's arrest!

---

hawked: offered goods for sale by shouting in the street

Glover jumped up. An arrest warrant could mean only one thing: slave catchers. What could he do? Even in free Wisconsin, the law was not on his side. He had seen other runaways put in chains and taken back to slavery.

Glover had one small hope. The door was latched. Maybe he could slip out the window and disappear into the woods.

But before Glover could reach the window, one of his friends, Nelson Turner, did an unbelievable, unthinkable thing. He pulled the latch and unlocked the door!

WHi Image ID 6270

Joshua Glover

Crash! The door flew open. In seconds, the cabin was filled with yelling and fighting. U.S. Marshal Cotton and his men pushed their way inside, followed by bounty-hunting slave catchers, a police officer from St. Louis, and the last face Joshua Glover ever wanted to see again. It was his master, Benami Garland.

Glover raised his fists to fight. But what could he do against swinging clubs and iron handcuffs? The men kicked and beat Glover. They threw him, bleeding and half-conscious, into the back of their wagon. The driver shouted to the horses and flicked the whip. Later, people spread the story that Nelson Turner received $100 for betraying his friend.

U.S. Marshal Cotton and his men knew that abolitionists in Racine would not stand by and watch a free citizen dragged back to slavery. They decided to drive Joshua Glover secretly to Milwaukee. Their plan was to hold him in jail, find a proslavery judge to sign the legal papers, and whisk him back to Missouri. Speed and darkness were on their side. No one and nothing seemed to be on Joshua Glover's side.

WHi Image ID 40122

Main Street in Racine, 1860

But Marshal Cotton and the slave catchers made one mistake. They forgot the people in Milwaukee who loved freedom. The Fugitive Slave Law of 1850 made it a crime to help a runaway slave. The slave catchers did not believe anyone would break the law for one black man.

By the next morning, news of Joshua Glover flashed through Milwaukee. People were outraged. A fugitive slave jailed in their city? Sherman Booth, the editor of the abolitionist newspaper, jumped on a horse and tore up and down the streets of Milwaukee like another Paul Revere. He shouted for people to assemble at the jail. Church bells began to ring from every corner of the city. A loud, angry crowd gathered. Release this man now! people demanded. Speeches rang out, and pistols fired into the air. Wisconsin was a free state, and these people weren't willing to let anything change that—not even the Fugitive Slave Law. With every hour, the crowd grew larger and louder and angrier.

Down in Racine, news of Joshua Glover's arrest spread like a prairie fire, hot and quick. If Racine's abolitionists had anything to say about it, Joshua Glover would not go back to slavery without a fight.

One hundred men rushed on board the steamship *Pacific*, headed for Milwaukee. There was not a minute to waste. If they didn't reach Milwaukee in time, they feared Joshua Glover would already be taken away. Men whipped off their jackets and grabbed shovels. In the breath-stealing heat below deck, they fed coal into the ship's boilers. Every minute counted. They had to reach Milwaukee in time.

WHi Image ID 9485

Sherman Booth

When the *Pacific* pulled to the Milwaukee shore, the Racine men stampeded down the docks to the Milwaukee jail. There, to their amazement, they found more than 1,000 people shouting for the release of Joshua Glover.

U.S. Marshal Cotton was in a terrible fix. His job was to **enforce** the Fugitive Slave Law. But the crowd outside the jail was growing bigger and more out of control by the minute. The men from the *Pacific* arrived with legal papers demanding that Joshua Glover be sent back to Racine. The papers even included arrest warrants charging Benami Garland and Marshal Cotton with **assault** for beating Joshua Glover.

Marshal Cotton did not see any way out. The Fugitive Slave Law was the law of the whole country. By that law, Joshua Glover wasn't a citizen with rights. He was a

---

enforce: to make sure a rule or law is obeyed
assault (uh **sawlt**): to attack someone or something violently

slave and Benami Garland's property. Joshua Glover was **legally** no different from a runaway dog. It was Marshal Cotton's job to make sure that "property" was returned. He must enforce the law!

The crowd roared. Fists pounded the air. What kind of law made slave catchers out of people who hated slavery? People said that an **unjust** law was better broken.

The crowd pushed and shoved outside the jail. Set him free! the crowd demanded. They wouldn't be slave catchers for anyone! One man ran up with a pickax. Others brought a piece of wood nearly 20 feet long. The crowd had talked and listened long enough. The Fugitive Slave Law was not the only thing about to be broken!

The heavy piece of wood became a battering ram. Boom! Again and again the men slammed it against the jail door. Crack! The pickax struck. The door splintered. Then it was pulled to pieces. Abolitionists pushed toward the jail. Everyone had one goal: free Joshua Glover. Marshal Cotton's men tried to push them back. The street was a battlefield.

All around, people shouted and pushed. The marshal's men threatened to shoot. Would someone die before Joshua Glover could be freed? The crowd pressed closer.

Like a tidal wave, people surrounded Joshua Glover. Strong arms pushed Marshal Cotton and his men away. The crowd poured onto Wisconsin Street, down East Water Street, and rumbled to a stop at Walker's Point Bridge. There, Glover was tossed into the back of John Messenger's wagon. "Drive, Messenger! Drive!" someone yelled. As the wagon tore down the street, police officers, Marshal Cotton's

---

legally: according to the law
unjust: not fair or right

men, slave catchers, and even Benami Garland chased after. Folks said later that it looked like the entire U.S. government running down the middle of the road.

John Messenger drove clear to Waukesha before he pulled his exhausted horses to a stop. Finally, Joshua Glover could raise his head. Glover did not realize it then, but he was about to climb aboard the Underground Railroad, headed to freedom.

During the next few days, slave catchers and the Underground Railroad played a dangerous game of hide-and-seek. Marshal Cotton and his men waved arrest warrants around like flags. Where is Glover? they demanded. Sherman Booth and other abolitionists were thrown in jail, and police and slave catchers threatened many free black people.

WHi Image ID 3399

Peter Thomas was an escaped slave who joined the 15th Wisconsin Volunteer Infantry in the Civil War. He settled in Racine after the war, just like Joshua Glover tried to do.

Meanwhile, the Underground Railroad set about its silent and secret work. Joshua Glover spent the first night in a barn belonging to the Tichenor family in Waukesha. Hiding by day and traveling only at night, he moved to Richard Ela's shop in Rochester and to Reverend and Mrs. Kinney's house in Racine. No one knows how many people hid Glover.

While the slave catchers threatened and hunted, the Underground Railroad waited and watched. Then one night, a steamship with an abolitionist captain arrived in Racine Harbor. Glover climbed into the back of a wagon, and an abolitionist friend drove to the docks. They kept in the shadows until Joshua Glover could sneak on board the ship.

Before morning, the great paddle wheel began to turn, and the steamship, with her precious hidden cargo, set off for Canada. Joshua Glover's final miles on the Underground Railroad had begun.

Joshua Glover finally did reach Canada and freedom. But back in Wisconsin, his rescue lit a wildfire. Sherman Booth was convicted of breaking the Fugitive Slave Law for his part in Glover's escape. He went to jail and was fined $2,460—about 8 years' pay!

When the federal judge declared Sherman Booth guilty, Wisconsin's **Supreme Court** declared him innocent. The Wisconsin judges rejected the Fugitive Slave Law because it denied people a fair trial. The federal court said Wisconsin must accept and enforce the Fugitive Slave Law. Again, Wisconsin's judges refused. The whole country watched in amazement as the new state of Wisconsin **defied** the federal government.

Finally, in 1861, President Buchanan **pardoned** Sherman Booth.

WHi Image ID 38129

Orasmus Cole was an antislavery judge on Wisconsin's Supreme Court. He helped declare Sherman Booth innocent when he rejected the Fugitive Slave Law.

---

supreme court: the most powerful court in a state or country
defied (di **fīd**): refused to obey
pardoned: forgave or excused from punishment

A Family's Journey

N

CANADA

Lake Superior

WISCONSIN TERRITORY

Green Bay

Lake Winnebago

Stockbridge Indian Nation

Lake Michigan

Lake Huron

MICHIGAN

Lake Erie

Mississippi River

IOWA TERRITORY

ILLINOIS

INDIANA

OHIO

Free States

VIRGINIA

St. Louis

MISSOURI

Ohio River

KENTUCKY

TENNESSEE

Slave States

ARKANSAS

Map by Amelia Janes, Earth Illustrated, Inc.

5

SECRET SERVICE

More than 150 years ago, Eliza and Jeremiah Porter were missionaries in Green Bay. In the early and middle 1800s, Green Bay was one of Wisconsin's largest cities. It was located where the Fox River meets Green Bay, and its harbor was busy. From the bell tower of the Porters' church, people could see beyond the town to miles of woods and water.

The Porters' door was always open to anyone sick, hungry, or just worn thin with loneliness after months and months of winter. So the Porters were not surprised when a letter arrived from a member of the Stockbridge band of the **Mohican** Indian Nation announcing some unusual visitors.

The Stockbridge band of the Mohicans had **migrated** from their homes in Stockbridge, Massachusetts, in the 1820s. Their first home in Wisconsin was the eastern shore of Lake Winnebago. They knew too well what it meant to be pushed out by the government taking their lands. That's why they had made the long journey to Wisconsin. Now it was their turn to help others on a journey to freedom.

Mohican (moh **hee** kuhn)
migrated: moved from one country or region to another

41

Freedom Train North

The letter to the Porters carried news that members of the Stockbridge band had hidden a family of fugitive slaves—a father and 3 young children. What had happened to the mother? No one knew. Slavery is cruel. She may have died, or even been sold away.

The Porters' church

Wherever people ran from slavery, slave catchers were always a danger, so the Stockbridge kept watch. Sure enough, bounty hunters were spotted sneaking around Stockbridge land. The fugitive slave family was no longer safe. Maybe the Underground Railroad could help. So a letter was sent to Green Bay, and the freedom train began to "move."

Eliza Chappell Porter told the story in a letter to her daughter. Eliza wrote, "A letter came from Mr. Goodell of Stockbridge saying that a father and his children had for some time enjoyed **refuge** in that Indian nation, but **pursuers** had discovered their resting place. . . . Would we receive them and send them to the steamboat on the coming Tuesday? Surely we could do that."

Would the Porters help? Of course. They knew Captain Stewart of the fine ship *Michigan* would take any fugitive slave to Canada. What could be simpler than hiding a family overnight and sneaking them on board a waiting ship? However,

refuge: protection or shelter
pursuer: a person chasing someone or something

the Porters soon learned that when slave catchers, reward money, and freedom were involved, nothing was simple.

"They did not arrive at the hour **appointed**," Mrs. Porter wrote. "But at midnight we were awakened by a knock at our window, and there stood the poor trembling father, and three cold hungry children. Our house was already full and the boat was not in port, and they feared the pursuers were on their track."

The Porters welcomed the family with hot food and a warm fire. Their guests' sad, hard story tumbled out as the Porters listened.

Somewhere in the South this father had stolen away with his 4 children. On foot, they managed to avoid **betrayers**, bloodhounds, and bounty hunters until they reached St. Louis, Missouri. Eliza and Jeremiah listened in horror as the father told his story. One child had become sick. Nothing the desperate man could do made any difference. His little one just grew sicker and sicker. The child died.

There was no time for tears. Slave catchers would not wait for them to **grieve**. The father had to bury his child and keep running. Somehow they covered the long miles to Wisconsin and found safety and kindness with the Stockbridge people. But even there, slave catchers found them. They were on the run again.

Mrs. Porter wondered what to do. The house was full, and other guests were expected. "Where can we hide them?" she wondered. "In the ice-house? In the side closets of the **parsonage**? I asked the God of all wisdom, love, and truth to direct."

---

appointed: chosen
betrayer: a person who turns against another
grieve: to feel very sad because someone has died
parsonage: the house provided by a church for its pastor

The answer came like a lightning flash. "That is the place!" Mr. Porter replied. "The **belfry!**"

Before the first morning sunlight, Eliza gathered food and blankets, and Jeremiah took the family to the church. Silently they crept inside and began to climb the narrow ladder to the bell tower. Higher and higher they climbed until they pushed open a trap door to a tiny room at the very top. They could see all of Green Bay from this treetop perch—streets and houses, kitchen gardens, shops, and barns. In the distance they saw the smokestacks of steamships and the docks where they hoped and prayed the *Michigan* would come to port.

But the *Michigan* did not come. Days of whispering and nights of waiting passed without a single sign of Captain Stewart or his ship. The lake was a dangerous place. Everyone understood that storms and fire had sunk steamers many times before. What would the Porters do if the *Michigan* never arrived? Every freedom worker in Green Bay was watching that dock.

Time must have passed so slowly. Hour after hour the children had to be as silent as stones. No one must suspect that people were hiding in the bell tower. Thursday, Friday, and Saturday passed, and the Porters began to worry about a new problem. Sunday morning the bell would ring, and the church would fill with people. What would the family do then?

---

belfry (bel free): the tower, or room in a tower, where a large bell is hung

Green Bay harbor around 1850

The question was answered by good news! At last, the steamer *Michigan* had been spotted heading into Green Bay harbor. Every freedom worker jumped into action. Deacon Kimball made tracks to Captain Stewart with a message that 4 extra passengers would be boarding. The Porters quietly led the father and children to the river, where an abolitionist friend rowed them out to the waiting ship.

From there, the Porters said, "Captain Stewart took them into his care." The steamship puffed its way north across Lake Michigan to Lake Huron, "to her Majesty's land of freedom": Canada. On the Canadian shore the grateful father fell on his knees to "kiss the free soil and give thanks to the Lord who had brought them out of the house of **bondage**."

◆　◆　◆　◆

This story is especially interesting because European American and American Indian abolitionists worked together. This had happened before in Wisconsin. Members of the Stockbridge and Brothertown nations and their non-Indian neighbors had met to start an antislavery society. One Stockbridge man named Collins Fowler said he was willing to die to see slavery ended. "Whatever others thought," Reverend Edward Mathews wrote, "he was willing to **testify** against slavery, even if for doing so his life should be **sacrificed**." At the meeting, a black man rose to speak. He had been a slave until he found safety with the Brothertown nation. In front of everyone he cried for his brothers and sisters still in slavery.

---

bondage (**bon** dij): slavery
testify: to state the truth or give evidence in court
sacrificed: given up for a reason

All abolitionists were courageous, but American Indian freedom workers were especially brave. Life was already filled with trouble for Indian people. Non-Indian settlement had pushed many Indian nations from their homelands. Then the U.S. government had pushed them onto **reservations**. Members of Indian nations risked even more trouble by protecting runaway slaves. So, the names Stockbridge and Brothertown have places of honor in the history of Wisconsin's Underground Railroad.

WHi Image ID 1909

The two men with their hands raised are Stockbridge Indians. They are joining the army to fight with the Union against slavery in the Civil War.

reservation: federal land reserved or set aside for Indian nations to live on

47

Journeys Overground and Underground

CANADA

Lake Superior

MINNESOTA

WISCONSIN

Lake Michigan

Lake Huron

MICHIGAN

Mississippi River

Waukesha
Milton
Janesville
Milwaukee
Racine

IOWA

Chicago

Emerald
Grove

OHIO

Free   States

ILLINOIS

INDIANA

Ohio River

MISSOURI

KENTUCKY

ARKANSAS

TENNESSEE

Slave States

Map by Amelia Janes, Earth Illustrated, Inc.

6

OVERGROUND, UNDERGROUND

Every house in Janesville was still and dark when Hiram and Eliza Foote heard a knock at their door. Since their home was one of the safe places called "stations" on the Underground Railroad, they were always ready for secret, late-night visitors.

Every **homesteader** in the county knew Hiram Foote as a pioneer preacher. He and Eliza moved from place to place. They preached in someone's barn one Sunday and a one-room cabin the next until folks scraped up enough money to put up a church building.

Hiram and Eliza built churches in the newborn towns of the Wisconsin Territory. However, they were also building stations and networks of workers on the Underground Railroad. So that night in Janesville, the Footes were not surprised to open their door to someone on the run from slavery—someone alone, afraid, and leaning on a crutch. His name was George.

---

homesteader: someone who has been given land to settle on and work by the U.S. government

Drawing of slave catchers shooting at slaves

Forty years later, Eliza Foote wrote down George's story. Somewhere between Illinois and the Wisconsin border, slave catchers had shot George as he fled. Bleeding and in pain, he somehow limped and crawled to an Underground Railroad station. Freedom workers cut the bullet from his leg and bandaged it. Then they hurried him on to the Footes' house as soon as he could walk. Time was precious because the slave catchers would not give up looking. They had shot him once and wouldn't hesitate to shoot again.

"Three lawyers who could be trusted came under cover of darkness for fear of proslavery laws, to interview our guest," Eliza wrote. Hiram and Eliza needed to be sure this man was truly a fugitive slave. Slave catchers would do anything for reward money. Someone might even pretend to be a runaway in order to betray freedom workers and hurt the Underground Railroad. But George was no betrayer. He was just a brave man desperate for freedom.

After weeks on the run, George needed sleep as much as food and bandages, so he stayed with the Footes for 2 days. Then, Eliza explained, "He was fed, clothed, and provided with a **satchel** that he might appear more like a northern tourist than a runaway slave." Dressed like a gentleman, who would guess that George was running from slavery? He would look like a **freedman** visiting relatives in Milwaukee or Racine. With this disguise, he went on to Lake Michigan where a steamship waited.

Even on board an abolitionist's ship, George was not completely safe. Hiram and Eliza would worry until he was free in Canada. So, as George left, Hiram handed him an envelope to be mailed when he arrived in Canada. The address read: *Reverend and Mrs. Hiram Foote, Janesville, Wisconsin, USA.* Then, they waited, hoping for good news. "In due time," Eliza wrote, the letter came, "which means as much to us as though containing an account of the journey. We knew George was safe."

---

satchel: a bag or small suitcase
freedman: a person who had been a slave and who bought, was given, or took his or her freedom

Hiram and Eliza Foote were church leaders in the Wisconsin towns of Janesville, Racine, Emerald Grove, Milton, and Waukesha. Everywhere Hiram preached the same simple message: love God, help your neighbor, and stand like a rock against slavery. It was no accident that *each* of these places was a stop on Wisconsin's Underground Railroad.

A half-day's wagon ride from Janesville is the little pioneer town of Milton. In Milton today, people can still see a most unusual station on Wisconsin's Underground Railroad, the Milton House Inn.

In 1819, Joseph Goodrich hiked into the hills of western New York with a bundle of clothes on his back, an ax in his hand, and 50 cents in his pocket. He and his sweetheart, Nancy Maxson, married and set up housekeeping in a log cabin with a dirt floor and a blanket for a door. Today, movies would make their life look like a romantic adventure. In reality it was endless, weary, sunup-to-sundown hard work. Their land was poor, and their best crop seemed to be field stones and tree stumps. Then, the rain stopped. **Drought** settled in. Wheat crumbled in the fields like old paper. So, in 1838, Joseph went west to Wisconsin. He had heard about Wisconsin's prairies and great stretches of oak and pine forest. Wisconsin land was cheap and good. If hard work could get them a farm, he and Nancy were ready for it.

When Joseph returned, the family loaded everything they owned into a wagon. Then Nancy, Joseph, their daughter, Jane, and son, Ezra, joined the thousands of

---

drought (drout): a long spell of very dry weather

WHi Image ID 39828

Milton House

pioneers on the road to the Wisconsin Territory. They spent the first summer in a one-room cabin in Milton, Wisconsin, with 13 people packed inside!

A **territorial** road passed through Milton. Joseph and Nancy Goodrich figured tired travelers would pay for soft beds and a good supper, so they built an inn. Soon stagecoaches were stopping at the Milton House, and those feather beds were filled with travelers headed to or from the big cities of Milwaukee and Chicago.

---

territorial (ter uh **tor** ee uhl): having to do with a particular land or region

The Goodriches were more than pioneers. They were also Seventh Day Baptists, Christian people of deep faith known from New York to the Mississippi River as rock-solid, no-**compromise** abolitionists. No penny of slavers' money was welcome in their offering boxes. No slave owners sat in their congregations. Seventh Day Baptists were warriors in the fight against slavery. When the chance came for the Goodriches to join the fight, they did not hesitate.

Joseph's brother, William, settled in Wisconsin too. He ran a ferry across the Rock River, **shuttling** wagons, people, and goods. On at least one occasion, he carried a human "parcel," a man named Andrew Pratt who had run from slavery.

Andrew Pratt had run from somewhere in Missouri just before the Civil War. He reached Illinois, thinking he would be safe. After all, Illinois was a free state. Or was it? Pratt did not know about "Black Laws" written to keep black people without jobs and money from settling in Illinois. But where would a fugitive slave get a job and money? So Andrew Pratt, who had come to Illinois to be free, was thrown in jail for the "crime" of being black and not having a job or money!

What happened then? Maybe Pratt was taken to the Wisconsin border and released. Maybe he escaped. Maybe abolitionists helped him. No one knows. But, about 5 years later, Ezra Goodrich, Joseph and Nancy's son, wrote Pratt's story.

---

compromise (**kom** pruh mız): to agree to accept something that is not exactly what you wanted
shuttling: regularly traveling back and forth along the same route

"Through the assistance of a **noble-hearted** Uncle of mine, William Goodrich," Ezra wrote, "Andrew Pratt was brought to the quiet and liberty loving little village of Milton." In fact, William Goodrich brought Pratt to his brother Joseph's inn in Milton, Wisconsin.

The Milton House tunnel where Andrew Pratt hid

Nancy and Joseph Goodrich never asked *if* they would help fugitive slaves, but *how*. In their tiny town, keeping secrets was hard. In a hotel where people arrived at any hour, it was almost impossible. How could they have hotel guests upstairs and other—secret—guests in the cellar? Fugitive slaves could not just knock on the hotel door. They needed a secret entrance, but what kind?

Joseph Goodrich did not let problems stand in his way. One idea led to another, until he had a bold, wild plan.

Just as the name Underground Railroad suggests, Joseph went *under the ground*. In back of the inn stood a tiny log cabin used for storage. Joseph cut a trapdoor in the cabin floor and began to dig. He scraped, shoveled, and hauled until he had dug a tunnel 50 feet long and 3 feet high—straight into the cellar of the Milton House Inn!

---

noble-hearted: idealistic, considerate

Freedom Train North

Andrew Pratt hid in the tunnel. When it was safe, Joseph sent him to a friend who needed a good farmhand. Over the next 5 years, Pratt went into business for himself. Later, he became a homesteader, plowing acres of prairie grass to "prove up," or pay for government land with hard work instead of money. By 1865, he had won the friendship and respect of many in Milton, including Ezra Goodrich.

Many years later, a torn piece of paper no bigger than a child's hand was found among the Goodrich family letters and diaries. The paper was the final piece of the story of Andrew Pratt and the Milton House tunnel. The paper read as follows:

> *Andrew Pratt came to J . . .*
>
> *in 1861 was cared for and . . .*
>
> *the underground passage, . . .*
>
> *him a job with David Plott . . .*
>
> *village where he worked & . . .*
>
> *Afterwards emigrated to . . .*
>
> *where he proved up on Gov. . . .*

The underground tunnel to the cellar of the Milton House Inn still exists and is part of the Milton Historical Society Museum. The Milton House is Wisconsin's only site on the **register** of National Historic **Landmarks** of the Underground Railroad.

One hundred fifty years ago, fugitive slaves crawled on hands and knees along a dirt passage barely wider than a man's shoulders. Today the tunnel has stone walls and a cement floor. But the chilly, underground darkness has not changed. Visitors' hearts still beat faster as they stare through the opening in the cabin floor and creep down the ladder. The darkness gives an unexpected shiver of fear, as though the tunnel itself remembers other long-ago visitors to the Milton House cellar.

---

register: a book in which names or official records are kept
landmark: an important building or place

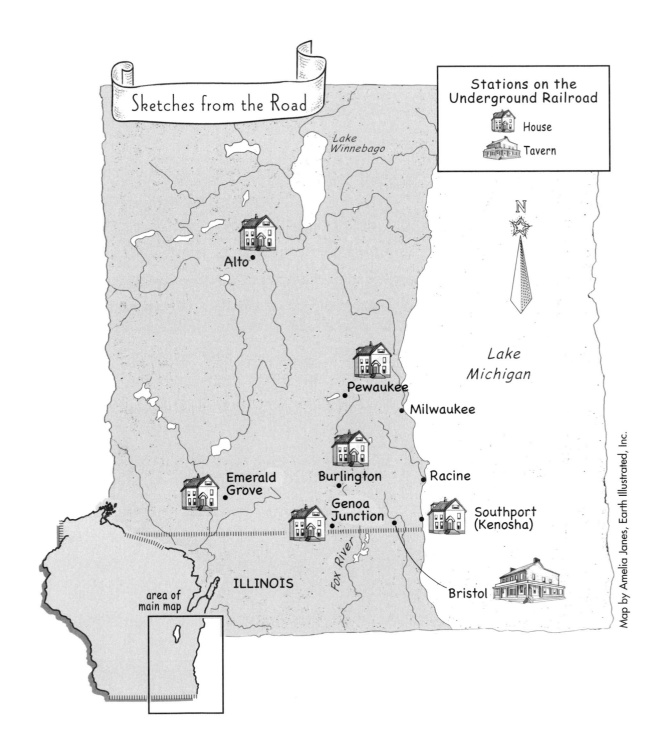

Sketches from the Road

Stations on the
Underground Railroad

House

Tavern

Lake
Winnebago

Alto

Lake
Michigan

N

Pewaukee

Milwaukee

Burlington

Racine

Emerald
Grove

Genoa
Junction

Southport
(Kenosha)

ILLINOIS

Fox River

Bristol

area of
main map

Map by Amelia Janes, Earth Illustrated, Inc.

7

SKETCHES FROM THE ROAD

*The stories in this chapter are incomplete. Only these sketches have **survived**, but together they help us understand more of the history of the Underground Railroad in Wisconsin.*

Hoofin' It to the Lake

In the days of the Underground Railroad, Kenosha was called Southport: *south* because it was near Wisconsin's southern border and *port* because Lake Michigan steamships stopped there. Kenosha was the first Underground Railroad station along Lake Michigan north of Illinois. Some fugitives made their way around Chicago and trekked north on foot—"hoofin' it." Others followed rivers and dirt roads from the Mississippi River into Wisconsin.

---

survived: stayed alive through a dangerous event

Freedom Train North

Whole families were freedom workers in Kenosha. Teenagers went on errands with secret "cargo" hidden in the back of the family's wagon. Children took blankets to a hidden guest or filled a basket with food for a hungry runaway. But first, even the youngest child had to learn the silent and secret ways of the Underground Railroad. One woman, Kate Deming, told her childhood story to her son, who wrote it down for us.

Kate Deming remembered strange goings-on at her home when she was just a little girl. She did not understand why Papa and Mama were whispering. Who were the strangers who came at night and left before breakfast? What was an Underground Railroad?

As she grew up, she *did* come to understand, and she, too, became a freedom worker. Her first job was to keep a secret. She knew about the "guests" in their attic, but she never, ever would tell—not even her best friend. People had already plotted to fire her papa from his job for preaching against slavery. If they knew he hid runaways, they would hand him over to the U.S. marshal without a second thought.

"Now Kate," her mother said, "don't tell any of the children at school today about the black man in the attic, or the officers may come and take him away, and they may perhaps put your father into prison."

For 2 or 3 days, Kate carried the awful, terrifying knowledge that her family was breaking the law by hiding fugitive slaves. When their "guest" finally slipped safely on board a steamship, Kate's whole family must have breathed a sigh of relief.

A Wisconsin home during the time of the Underground Railroad

WHi Image ID 30027

Some of the Demings' neighbors had secrets of their own. William Smith was a teenager when his father told him, "Don't go to the barn tonight. Father will do the chores." William woke in the morning to find his horse tired and the wagon wheels muddy. Yet at breakfast his father smiled and chatted and teased the little ones as though nothing had happened. William was not fooled for a minute. Father had gone somewhere in the middle of the night. Behind his pasted-on smile, he looked worried and tired. What secret was he keeping?

William's answer came weeks later. Night had barely settled in when Mother scooted the little ones to bed and sent William to the kitchen to fix food. Fixing supper at bedtime? Suddenly, the kitchen door opened. Four people—a father, mother, and 2 children—were pushed inside. William did not have to ask who they were. Their worried faces told him everything. They were African American people running from slavery.

The family stayed only long enough to eat and squeeze into the back of the Smiths' wagon. Without a word, William's father flicked the reins and guided the wagon down the gravel driveway. William watched them disappear into the darkness.

The next morning, William came to the breakfast table as usual. He smiled and chatted and teased his little brothers as though nothing had happened. Just like his father and mother, William, too, had become part of the Underground Railroad.

Kellogg's Tavern

Theodore Fellows had made the trip from Genoa Junction to Kenosha so many times with his father that he could practically drive the roads in his sleep. They always drove all day, slept at James Kellogg's tavern in Bristol, and reached Kenosha the next morning.

Genoa Junction was so small that if the neighbor's pig had a litter, folks considered it major news. Kenosha was a *real* city, with wide streets and long piers stretching like fingers out into Lake Michigan. For Theodore, a trip to Kenosha was an exciting chance to hear real news and see real sights. This time he was going alone.

WHi Image ID 35343

Kellogg's Tavern

Theodore loaded hundred-pound bags of wheat into the wagon. The job was a sweaty backbreaker, so he was glad when his father offered to help. But then his father began arranging the bags around the wagon sides with an open square in the center. Theodore stared. What was his father doing?

"It rides better that way," Father explained. Theodore had loaded wagons since he was old enough to lift a grain sack. But this was the first time his father had done such a thing. Odd.

The next morning the bags of wheat were covered with a large canvas cloth. Theodore's father handed him his lunch and gave him very particular, unusual instructions. Theodore was to eat down by the Fox River. No **dawdling**, Father said. "Don't speak to anyone unless necessary, and then say nothing but 'yes' and 'no.'" And he must reach Kellogg's Tavern by dark.

Imagine. Theodore's father was acting so strangely. First, there was the peculiarly loaded wagon, then the stern looks and instructions to keep quiet. Something was wrong. The best part of a trip was to talk and hear the news from folks along the way, and Theodore's father knew it. None of it made sense. Still, Theodore knew better than to question his father, so he obeyed the unusual orders.

That night at Kellogg's Tavern, James Kellogg was waiting in the driveway. He signaled the wagon straight into the barn and kicked the door shut. Without a word, Kellogg pulled back the canvas cloth and began to unload the wagon. What was he doing? Then, Theodore was absolutely, completely amazed. Mr. Kellogg pulled a *man* out from under the bags of wheat and hustled him away toward the house.

Suddenly, everything made sense. His father had loaded the wheat and ordered Theodore to keep to himself because a fugitive slave was hidden in the back of the wagon!

---

dawdling: doing something slowly, wasting time

Back home in Genoa Junction, Theodore Fellows's father told him about the Underground Railroad. This surprise at Kellogg's Tavern was probably not the only time the Fellows family made the trip to Kenosha with their wagon carrying cargo much more valuable than wheat.

Burlington

Dr. Edward Galusha Dyer was a "double abolitionist." That is, he not only hid runaways in his home, but he was also a leader in the work against slavery. When Caroline Quarlls and Lyman Goodnow needed money for their journey to Canada, Dr. Dyer collected money from other abolitionists right on the sidewalk in Burlington. He also named the street in front of his house "Liberty Avenue" and was famous for saying, "Can liberty and slavery long dwell together? Which side shall we be on? Surely we will be for liberty."

Courtesy of the Burlington Historical Society

Dr. Edward Dyer

Alto: On the Prairie

In 1900, J. B. Pond remembered, "My father kept an underground station. Many a night I have slept out on the prairie with some runaway slaves, with Father and the neighbors protecting them against the United States marshal. I found myself, when eighteen years of age, carrying a **Sharps rifle** in 1856 with **John Brown**, in Kansas."

John Brown was a radical abolitionist.

Courtesy of Library of Congress, LC-USZ62-106337

Pewaukee: Sleeping by the Stove

In 1926, Mollie Maurer Kartak described a time when she was a little girl and an older black man came to her parents' house. He was "carrying a small child, was brought into the house, fed, and put to sleep on the floor near the kitchen stove. During the night my father took a load of hay to some man quite a distance away. Years later, my mother told me that the colored man and child were slaves whom my father had smuggled away under cover of the hay to the next station of the 'Underground Railway.'"

Sharps rifle: a weapon common in the Civil War era
John Brown: an American abolitionist who worked hard and fought with weapons against slavery

Emerald Grove: Race to Racine

It was a crisp, red-and-gold Wisconsin autumn day in 1855 in the little crossroads town of Emerald Grove. At their home, Deacon and Mrs. Cheney set hot dishes on the table. As the family ate, a covered carriage rumbled up the drive. Sunday visitors, what a surprise! The children tumbled out the door and surrounded the carriage. They saw that rain flaps were lowered to hide the passengers. Even 40 years later, one of those children, Russell Cheney Jr., remembered what happened next.

Mr. Leonard, a friend from Beloit, jumped from the carriage seat and called out to Deacon Cheney. The children could hardly believe what they heard. Inside the wagon were 6 fugitive slaves: a husband, wife, and 4 children. A slave hunter was following close behind!

The Cheney children crowded closer. Were there really runaway slaves in the wagon? While the adults spoke in low, serious tones, the children lifted the rain flaps and peeked inside. Four other children stared back at them.

In another place and time, the children might have become friends. But on that day slavery and slave catchers stood between them.

The adults decided on a plan: Deacon Cheney took the family to the home of a trusted abolitionist friend, Simeon Reynolds. If they left immediately and raced to Racine, they could catch the outgoing steamer and leave the slave hunter empty-handed.

That was exactly what Simeon Reynolds did. For 60 miles, Reynolds dodged potholes and mud as he flew down the territorial road to the Racine docks. Not long after, freedom workers sent back the "glad news" that the family was safe in Canada.

Jacob Green's Journeys

CANADA

Lake Superior

WISCONSIN

Lake Michigan

Lake Huron

MICHIGAN

Toronto

Lake Ontario

Niagara Falls

Lake Erie

NEW YORK

Utica

N

IOWA

ILLINOIS

Free States

Mississippi River

INDIANA

Sandusky

Cleveland

OHIO

PENNSYLVANIA

NEW JERSEY

DELAWARE

MARYLAND

VIRGINIA

Ohio River

KENTUCKY

MISSOURI

NORTH CAROLINA

TENNESSEE

SOUTH CAROLINA

ARKANSAS

MISSISSIPPI

ALABAMA

GEORGIA

Slave States

ATLANTIC OCEAN

Key

⇨ Escaped and captured

➡ Escaped to freedom

LOUISIANA

FLORIDA

New Orleans

Gulf of Mexico

Map by Amelia Janes, Earth Illustrated, Inc.

8

OPEN THE WINDOW AND JUMP!

In 1848, Captain Gilman Appleby of the steamship *Sultana* became a Wisconsin hero. Out on Lake Erie, hundreds of miles from the docks of Racine and Milwaukee, he saved a fugitive slave named Jacob Green.

Jacob Green just would not give up his freedom dreams. Four times he ran from slavery. The first time, he escaped from Kentucky. The second time, he escaped from New Orleans. A third time, he ran away from Maryland, and finally, from Kentucky again. He ran from cruel masters and kind ones. He ran from big plantations and riverboats. Each time he was caught. Each time he was whipped and sold. Then, in a new place with a new master, he would pretend to be an *obedient* slave. But all the while, he was keeping his eyes open for a chance to run. When that chance came, north he went again!

Reward posters like this one encouraged people to turn in runaway slaves.

---

obedient (oh **bee** dee uhnt): doing what one is told to do

Freedom Train North

Once he rubbed **manure** on his feet. He hoped that the smell would fool the bloodhounds following him. Another time, with slave catchers chasing him, he raced through the back door of an Irish family's **shanty**. He ran across the kitchen and out the front, knocking the whole family to the floor as he passed. He crawled into a cellar and spent the night squeezed inside a chimney. Still another time he pretended he could not hear or speak. Slave catchers decided he was "a madman" and let him go. He didn't wait a minute longer than necessary before heading north again.

He found help from free blacks on the Underground Railroad. They smuggled him into the dark hold of a Mississippi riverboat where he burrowed under bales of cotton. From boat to wagon, back road to city street, he traveled until he reached Utica, New York. Canada was almost in sight. Almost.

With Canada only a day's journey away, Jacob Green saw a face he had hoped never to see again. His former owner from Kentucky! Green turned to run. The man screamed for help, and a dozen people came running. Strong arms grabbed Green and held him until police arrived with **ankle irons** and handcuffs. Jacob Green was caught again and thrown in jail.

"While in prison," Green wrote later, "a complaint was made that a fugitive slave was placed in irons, **contrary** to the law." News of Green's capture spread. Angry crowds of abolitionists protested outside the jail. "On the Monday following I was taken on board the steamship *Sultana* bound for Sandusky, Ohio, and on my way

---

manure: animal waste put on land to help crops grow better
shanty: roughly built hut or cabin, often made of wood
ankle irons: iron cuffs worn around the ankle to prevent a slave from escaping
contrary: opposite

WHi Image ID 5678

A steamboat similar to the *Sultana*

there, the Black people in large numbers made an attempt to rescue me. And so desperate was the attack that several officers were wounded, [but] the attempt failed. I was placed in the cabin."

Locked in and tied up, Jacob Green could only wait. He knew that in a few hours he would be shoved on board a train, chained to the wall, and shipped back to Kentucky.

Gilman Appleby was captain of the *Sultana*. He had watched police wrestle Jacob Green on board his ship. He watched as they pushed Green into the captain's cabin. He could not help but hear the crowd roar and shout, demanding Green's release.

Captain Appleby saw it all and did nothing. He stood by while Green was tied up. Just one more uncaring white man, or so it seemed.

Actually, Gilman Appleby cared so much he could have wept. But he could not show it. He had to keep a secret, and nothing was more important—not even Jacob Green's freedom. The secret? Gilman Appleby was a Wisconsin freedom worker who used his beautiful new ship to smuggle fugitive slaves to Canada.

What could the captain do? Hundreds of miles away in Wisconsin, he would have had abolitionist friends nearby and ready to help. But on the shore of Lake Erie, he was alone.

Alone or not, secret or no secret, Appleby would not let his ship be used for slave-catching. Not while he had any power to stop it. He would help Jacob Green, of course. He just needed a chance, a plan, and a bit of luck.

Jacob Green wrote, "At dinner time the steamboat started and had about half a mile to go before she got into the lake, and on the way, the captain came down to me and cautiously asked me if I could swim."

Swim? A person could freeze to death in Lake Erie in the middle of November. No matter. Jacob Green said he could swim—and would—so the captain untied him.

"He told me to stand close by a window," Green continued. "And when the paddle wheels ceased I must jump out. I stood ready, and as soon as the wheels ceased I made a spring and jumped." Down, down, down he fell. Freezing water swelled over him. It was bone-aching, heart-stopping cold. Water that cold stabs like needles and sucks the breath from your body. Jacob Green fought his way to the surface and gasped to pull air into his lungs. Then he began to swim.

Everyone has heard the phrase "run for your life." Well, Jacob Green *swam* for his life. When Captain Appleby saw Green in the water, he gave the signal to start the ship's engines again. Smoke poured from the stacks, and the great paddle wheel began to turn.

In the water, Green had to pull with every ounce of his strength just to keep from being sucked under by the force of the paddles. As he **flailed** and kicked away from the boat he heard his former owner shout, "Here, here, stop, Captain! Stop!"

The owner yelled and waved his arms. Soon every person on deck knew a runaway slave was swimming to freedom. Passengers pressed against the railing and shouted as Jacob Green struggled toward shore. If the steamer had stopped, Green would have had no hope. But Captain Appleby did not say a word, and he refused to stop the ship. By the time Green reached the shore, the *Sultana* was gone.

Jacob Green **staggered** ashore near Cleveland, Ohio. He was shivering, numb, and half-frozen. A crowd of abolitionists hurried him away. But even then his story was not finished.

Before Jacob Green finally became a free man, he was discovered, arrested, and sold once more in Kentucky, back where he had started. But, even then, he didn't give up his dream of freedom.

Green acted like an obedient slave for almost a year. He bowed and smiled and said, "Yes, master," to his new owner. But all the time he was waiting for another chance to run.

---

flailed: moved, swung, or beat
staggered: walked unsteadily

A dock along the Ohio River

That chance came one day when Green was ordered to drive his master's daughter to the city. Instead of driving to the city, he stopped and tied the young woman to a tree with her own **shawl**. Then he jumped back in the wagon, and the horse **sprinted** for the Ohio River. At the river, he saw ships, docks, and black men loading and unloading freight. Green **hoisted** a trunk onto his shoulder and walked right on board a steamship as if he'd been a **dockhand** all his life. Once inside the ship, he hid under bales of cotton. The ship traveled to New York.

In New York, Jacob Green made his last escape with the help of the Underground Railroad. To fool slave hunters, he dressed as a woman! Freedom

---

shawl: a piece of soft material worn over the shoulders or around the head
sprinted: ran fast for a short distance
hoisted: lifted something heavy
dockhand: someone who works where ships load and unload cargo

workers gave him women's clothes. Wearing long skirts, gloves, and a veil, and carrying $12 in his pocket, he crossed Niagara Falls and headed to Toronto, Canada. There, Jacob Green said, at last, "I sang my song of deliverance."

The name Gilman Appleby and the *Sultana* were not alone on Wisconsin's honor role of abolitionist steamship captains and their ships. In 1896, Racine freedom worker A. P. Dutton listed these captains and their floating "stations" on Wisconsin's Underground Railroad.

- The *Madison*
- The *Niagara*
- The *Missouri*
- The *Keystone State*
- All General Reed's ships
- Captain Stewart of the *Michigan*
- Captain Steel of the *Galena*
- Captain Appleby of the *Sultana*
- Captain Kilsey of the *Chesapeake*

A. P. Dutton said more than 100 fugitive slaves were sent to freedom in Canada from the steamer docks in Racine alone. For those people and others too, freedom waited across the waters of Lake Michigan and Lake Huron. For them, the Underground Railroad was not a "freedom train" but a "freedom ship," making the journey from the ports of Wisconsin to Canada.

Fugitive Slaves and the Union Army

CANADA

N

Lake Superior

MINNESOTA

WISCONSIN

Lake Michigan

Lake Huron

Fond du-Lac   Lake Winnebago

MICHIGAN

Lake Erie

IOWA

Chicago

Free States

INDIANA

OHIO

ILLINOIS

MISSOURI

Ohio River

KENTUCKY

Slave States

Cairo

TENNESSEE

ARKANSAS

Fort Pillow

ALABAMA

MISSISSIPPI

GEORGIA

9
OPEN HEARTS, OPEN HANDS

A thin, tired-eyed woman pried open a missionary barrel in the **Union Army** chaplain's tent. She ran her hands over little flower-print dresses and rough cotton trousers and whispered a prayer of thanks for the Michigan girls and women who had sent them. She could have had 10 more barrels of clothing and that still would not be enough. So many fugitives had come to Fort Pillow, Tennessee, that Laura Haviland wondered if every slave on every plantation in the entire South had run. But every day, more former slaves kept arriving.

One by one she pulled clothes from the barrel and handed them to a long line of shivering children. Ragged flour-sack dresses and pants were slipped off, and clean, bright clothes took their place. Suddenly, the tent exploded with the squealing laughter of little girls. Years later Laura Haviland still recalled that joyful scene.

"One little girl exclaimed in surprise, 'Oh, Milla, my dress has a pocket, and see what I found,' as she drew out a rag doll two inches long. Then a dozen other little girls . . . found similar treasures. . . . All were on tip-toe with excitement."

Union Army: the military that fought for the northern states during the Civil War

People ran from slavery by the thousands as the Civil War heated up, and Union troops pushed farther and farther south. Individuals and groups, whole families, or even all the slaves on entire plantations fled to freedom.

These refugees from slavery were ragged, hungry, and tired. After waiting all their lives to be free, the sight of Union-blue uniforms and the **Stars and Stripes** flying overhead drew them like a candle in a long, dark tunnel.

Courtesy of Library of Congress, LC-DIG-cwpb-04294

Some African Americans finally got the opportunity to fight for the Union.

Stars and Stripes: the flag of the United States

Fugitive slaves came to get help. But, they also came to give it. Men said, Give us guns, and we will fight! They were willing to die for their freedom. But often they were not allowed to fight because they were black. Nevertheless, they were willing to help in any way they could. These fugitive slaves dug **trenches**, cooked food, washed laundry, and hauled firewood. Some of them became spies. Some of these spies even returned to the South to learn secret information about the **Confederate** plans.

But Union Army commanders did not know what to do with so many people. Food was so scarce that Union soldiers were stealing chickens and picking corn right out of the fields to feed themselves. How could the army possibly feed hundreds and hundreds of fugitives too?

Many churches helped. They sent freedom workers and supplies. Abolitionist women who could not fight slavery with guns took needles and thread and made clothing. And yes, Michigan girls really did stitch **miniature** rag dolls as a sweet surprise for other little girls to discover in the pockets of their new dresses.

Missionaries like Jeremiah and Eliza Porter, who had once hidden a father and 3 children in their church bell tower in Green Bay, Wisconsin, came as volunteers. Eliza nursed and cooked. Jeremiah and Reverend James Rogers from Fond du Lac signed on as chaplains.

---

trench: a long, narrow ditch used to protect soldiers in battle
Confederate (kuhn **fed** ur uht): having to do with the South during the Civil War
miniature (**min** ee uh chur): smaller than the usual size

Drawing of fugitive slaves leaving the South

James Rogers was put in charge of thousands of fugitive slaves in a crowded army camp in Cairo, Illinois. He had never seen so many human beings in his life.

"On Sunday just before sunset, over five hundred came in one body," Rogers wrote in his journal. Monday, "before breakfast was finished, another crowd of eleven hundred came to my quarters. It seemed as if the whole slave population were really fleeing."

Mothers with babies, **orphaned** children, strong men, and sick and old people lined up outside Reverend Rogers's tent. From sunrise to midnight, Reverend Rogers worked like 10 men. An empty tent became a school where former slaves crowded together, learning to read. Wash boilers were hung over open fires to cook cornmeal or wild-rabbit stew. Every night Rogers collapsed on his cot, knowing more people would come in the morning. This could not go on!

In some camps the gates were **barred** and hundreds of fugitive slaves sent away. We're here to fight a war, not operate a refugee camp, commanders grumbled. Some soldiers protested. They had come to fight slavery, not send people back to it. But orders were orders.

Abolitionists were horrified. How could the Union send innocent people back to slavery? Orders might be orders, but wrong was also *wrong*. Then they found a way around the orders using the army's own rules.

The army orders said "No refugees." So abolitionists decided fugitive slaves weren't refugees, they were **contraband**. Contraband was anything useful to an army, from corn in a farmer's field to blankets on the shelves of a general store.

Fugitive slaves were useful. The army was desperate for workers. So when orders came to turn fugitive slaves away, soldiers like Reverend Rogers refused. What fugitive slaves? Reverend Rogers only saw contraband!

---

orphaned: without any parents
barred: blocked to keep someone out
contraband (kon truh band): goods brought illegally from one place to another

Courtesy of Library of Congress, LC-DIG-cwpb-01005

A group of "contrabands" at a Union army camp in Virginia

Newly freed people helped the Union in another way. Reverend Rogers knew that back in Wisconsin, women and children struggled to keep farms running while their men fought as soldiers. In Illinois he saw thousands of former slaves ready and willing to work. Would people in Fond du Lac hire them? They would, and they did!

Plans were set, and people volunteered. Then, early one morning, 75 men, women, and children boarded a train in Cairo, Illinois, bound for Fond du Lac, Wisconsin. One of those children was 15-year-old Frances Shirley.

Frances huddled in the train car with everything she owned bundled in her lap. Before her family ran away, she had spent her whole life on Master Harris's plantation far away in Alabama. Now she was surrounded by strangers headed to an unknown place called Wisconsin. Imagine the questions tumbling through her mind. Was the North really filled with snow and wild animals like Master Harris had always claimed? Would she freeze ice-solid in winter? Would white folks in Wisconsin pay her to work, or would they just force her into slavery again?

On October 21, 1862, the train puffed into the Fond du Lac station. Outside, the leaves were golden, and the air was chilly. White faces peered into the windows of the train. Strangers. Some smiled. Others scowled and muttered. Frances saw supper laid out on long tables. Now she would find the answers to all those troublesome questions.

After supper the adults talked about jobs. Men were hired as field hands. Women found work as housekeepers or laundresses. Frances Shirley got a job as a "baby girl," helping Mrs. Gould with her little ones. Imagine, not long before, Frances had been stuffed in a train car in Cairo, Illinois, without a penny to her name. Now she had a paying job!

After the Civil War, Frances Shirley and her family stayed in Fond du Lac. She married, and her children grew up playing on Dixie Street along the Fond du Lac River and singing in the Freedman's Union Church choir. In 1935, the city honored Frances Shirley's 88th birthday. She lived to be one of the last people in Wisconsin to have been born a slave.

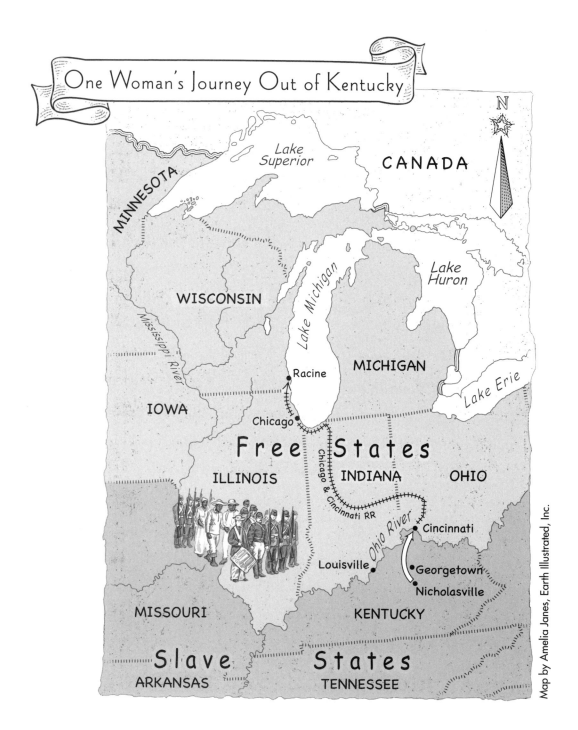

One Woman's Journey Out of Kentucky

N

CANADA

Lake Superior

MINNESOTA

WISCONSIN

Lake Michigan

Lake Huron

MICHIGAN

Lake Erie

Mississippi River

Racine

IOWA

Chicago

Free States

ILLINOIS

INDIANA

Chicago & Cincinnati RR

OHIO

Ohio River

Cincinnati

Louisville

Georgetown

Nicholasville

MISSOURI

KENTUCKY

Slave States

ARKANSAS

TENNESSEE

10

SOLDIER HEROES OF THE UNDERGROUND RAILROAD

It was October of 1862. Flags waved and voices shouted as the 22nd Wisconsin Volunteers marched through the streets of Racine. The 22nd Wisconsin Volunteers were known as the Abolition Regiment. Everyone cheered for them as they passed. Sweethearts cried. Hats and white lace handkerchiefs flew into the air as the soldiers marched away. Every last soldier was a Wisconsin man. Colonel William Utley rode at their head. The gold buttons gleamed on his Union-blue jacket. It was a proud day.

Everyone knew William Utley. He was not a **professional** soldier. But his fierce **loyalty** to his men earned their loyalty in return. Even in 1862, early in the Civil War, Wisconsin soldiers had earned a **reputation** as furious fighters. Wisconsin men died in nearly every place the war was fought.

People cheered as the men of the 22nd Wisconsin left for war. Before these young men marched home again, they fought terrible battles. All too soon Colonel Utley's men became **blood brothers** with every other Wisconsin regiment, who were both killing and dying.

---

professional: a member of a profession, such as teacher, doctor, nurse, or lawyer
loyalty: support or faithfulness to one's country, family, friends, or beliefs
reputation (rep yoo **tay** shuhn): a person's worth or character, as judged by other people
blood brother: a person who has sworn to treat another as his brother

WHi Image ID 24962

The 22nd Wisconsin crossing the Ohio River on their way to Camp Nelson

The 22nd Wisconsin was ordered to Nicholasville, Kentucky. There they trained, **drilled**, and learned to fight. They were willing to fight, even die. But they weren't willing to accept what they found in Nicholasville.

In 1862, Kentucky was a **border state**. The people of the state had mixed loyalties. Some folks fought for the Union. Others owned slaves and hated **Yankees**. Utley's men grumbled as they set up camp in ankle-deep mud, **scrounged** for food, and slept on haystacks. But mud and growling stomachs were not the worst of it.

---

drilled: did something over and over again in order to learn it well
border state: one of the slave states of Delaware, Maryland, Virginia, Kentucky, and Missouri that were next to the free states of the North during the Civil War
Yankee: someone born or living in the northern states
scrounged: collected things with difficulty

Across the fence from them, the freedom-loving men of Wisconsin's Abolition Regiment saw slaves working the fields!

Slaves? Most of Utley's soldiers were abolitionists. They were shocked. Wasn't Kentucky in the Union? Wasn't the Union against slavery? The soldiers' grumbling became a roar. They had not left their wives and families to watch slaves work in the next field!

It was true that Kentucky was part of the Union. Abraham Lincoln *had* written the **Emancipation Proclamation** on September 22, 1862. However, his proclamation freed people held in slavery only in the states "in **rebellion**." In this case, "in rebellion" meant *southern* states that had left the Union. Also, the Proclamation didn't take effect until January 1 of the following year.

Courtesy of the National Archives, 299998

The first page of the Emancipation Proclamation

Emancipation Proclamation (i man si **pay** shun prok luh **may** shun): a document signed by Abraham Lincoln in 1863 declaring the slaves free
rebellion: armed fight against the government

Freedom Train North

Kentucky was a loyal Union state. It was also a slave state. What could President Lincoln do? If he freed Kentucky slaves, the state might leave the Union to join the Confederacy. The Union could not afford to lose more states. President Lincoln had to compromise. In the end, the Union kept Kentucky, and Kentucky kept its slaves.

The angry roar of the Abolition Regiment was only the beginning. Soon, William Utley and his men would have to stand against **Brigadier General** Gilmore, the **chief justice** of Kentucky's supreme court, and the entire Union Army command!

A sign of trouble came one November day when a beautiful young fugitive slave woman crept into the 22nd Wisconsin camp. She asked to see the commander. Wisconsin soldiers took her to Colonel Utley and listened in horror as she told her story.

The young woman wept. She was only 18 years old. Her master had made plans to sell her to a man who bought beautiful young women as slaves to entertain the customers in his gambling house. The girl said she would rather die than be grabbed by drunken men. She begged the 22nd Wisconsin for help.

Colonel Utley and every Wisconsin soldier knew the brigadier general's orders. Hiding runaway slaves was forbidden. Fugitives must be sent back to their masters.

The roar of the 22nd Wisconsin became a thundering *No!* Orders or no orders, they would not let this girl be taken. "We came here as freemen from a free State, to defend and support a free government," said Colonel Utley. "We have nothing to

---

brigadier general: an officer in the U.S. Army, Air Force, or Marine Corps ranking above colonel and below major general
chief justice: the head of the state's or country's court system

Courtesy of the University of Kentucky Archives

Camp Nelson

do with slavery." No one could order them to do slave catchers' work. Not even the brigadier general.

The young woman's master stormed into the camp. He also knew the general's orders. He demanded his slave's return. The men managed to hide her among the supplies. But with an angry slave owner on one side and the brigadier general on the other, Colonel Utley decided the best plan was to sneak the young woman out of camp to a station on the Underground Railroad. So that's what the 22nd Wisconsin did!

About one o'clock the next morning, 2 farmers wearing civilian clothes whispered a password to the guards and drove their wagon out the front gate of the Nicholasville camp. The guards didn't look twice. Civilians often came to the camps. Maybe these men just stayed on for a bottle of whiskey and a late-night hand of poker with some soldiers.

Freedom Train North

If the guards had looked closer, they might have seen something familiar about the driver and his companion. If they had searched the hay-filled wagon, they would have seen even more.

The 2 "farmers" were really soldiers from the 22nd Wisconsin: **Sergeant** Jesse Berch from Racine and Corporal Frank Rockwell from Hudson. As soon as the wagon rattled over the hill, a scruffy-looking "soldier boy" pushed out from under the hay. The wagon, with its 3 passengers, traveled nearly 100 miles to Cincinnati, Ohio, straight up to the front door of Levi Coffin's house.

Levi and Catherine Coffin were peaceable Quakers. But across the Union and even in Wisconsin, they were known as fierce fighters against slavery. Levi Coffin was often called the president of the Underground Railroad.

Sergeant Berch, Corporal Rockwell, and the "soldier boy" dashed up to his house. In the daylight, anyone could see the "boy" was **biracial**, with creamy-brown skin. Even in free Ohio they could not risk being seen.

Levi Coffin opened the door. From the entryway Berch and Rockwell could see guests chatting in the **parlor**. They nervously whispered a message from Colonel Utley. Then, as calmly as if strange soldiers from Kentucky knocked on his door every day, Levi Coffin ordered Rockwell and Berch to take a seat and sent the "boy" upstairs with Mrs. Coffin.

---

sergeant (**sahr** juhnt): an officer in the U.S. Army or Air Force who is second in command of a small group of soldiers
biracial (bɪ **ray** shuhl): part one race and part another
parlor: a formal living room used for receiving guests

Levi Coffin wrote the rest of the story in his journal. "Next morning the soldier boy came down **transformed** into a young lady of **modest** manners and pleasing appearance." A young lady? Of course! The "soldier boy" was neither a soldier nor a boy! Colonel Utley's plan had succeeded. Back in Kentucky, that Lexington slaver was still searching for the young woman who had run away. Let him search! Let him shout and complain about losing a $1,700 slave to those thieving Yankee soldiers. Let him turn all Nicholasville upside down, because Jesse Berch and Frank Rockwell had taken his valuable "property" to Cincinnati, Ohio, right under everyone's noses!

Frank Rockwell and Jesse Berch with the brave young slave woman

---

transformed: greatly changed
modest: not boastful

91

Levi Coffin wrote, "Not **content** with **escorting** her to a free State, these brave young men **telegraphed** to Racine, Wisconsin, and made arrangements for their friends there to receive her." Coffin drove the young woman to a train station. Then he offered his arm as she boarded the first-class car. "She was nicely dressed and wore a veil, presenting the appearance of a white lady," Coffin recalled. As the train puffed out of the Cincinnati station, Berch and Rockwell raised their hats in salute. They knew that the brave young woman would soon arrive safely in Racine.

Berch and Rockwell returned to the 22nd Wisconsin the following Friday night. It had been more than a week since they had whispered that password and slipped out of Nicholasville. Cheering began the minute they jumped from the wagon. Soldiers hollered and tossed their hats into the air. Berch and Rockwell were 2 Wisconsin farm boys who had become heroes to the men of the Abolition Regiment.

While Berch and Rockwell were gone, the 22nd Wisconsin and other regiments like the 19th Michigan had taken in and hidden more fugitives. Colonel Utley continued to stand firm. No number of threats or orders could force him to give up the fugitive slaves hidden in his camp. More slave owners, including the chief justice of Kentucky's supreme court, came to the camp demanding their slaves. Each time, William Utley refused. Each time his men agreed. They were freedom fighters, not slave catchers. And besides, they were *Wisconsin* men; they would not retreat!

Finally, the Kentucky **politicians** and slave owners hatched a plan. Reverend George Bradley, chaplain of the 22nd Wisconsin, wrote the details in his journal.

---

content: happy and satisfied
escorting: accompanying someone, especially for protection
telegraphed: sent a message using a code of electrical signals sent by wire or radio
politician (pol uh **tish** uhn): someone who runs for or holds a government office, such as a senator

WHi Image ID 2248

These three men were abolitionists. On the right is Levi Coffin, "the president of the Underground Railroad."

Regiment by regiment, the newly-trained troops were ordered to the battlefront. First, the 19th Michigan regiment was ordered to Georgetown, Kentucky. As they reached the city, 40 men with drawn pistols rushed toward them. Fugitives from slavery were hidden among the soldiers. Every one was taken at gunpoint.

Other regiments where fugitives were protected were stopped. Every fugitive was snatched and dragged away. Finally, the Nicholasville camp was almost empty. Only the 22nd Wisconsin was left. The army's plan was clear as a bull's-eye on the side of a barn. Divide and conquer. The army command and the Kentucky politicians figured one regiment alone could not keep slave owners from reclaiming their "property."

Orders came for the 22nd Wisconsin to report to the docks in Louisville. A friend took Colonel Utley aside with a terrible warning. Every fugitive slave had been taken by force from the other regiments. He said men in Louisville "declared they would die rather than let the 22nd Wisconsin leave the state" with even one fugitive slave. Sheriffs, slave catchers, slave owners, and Kentucky politicians lined the streets of Louisville. The trap was laid, and the 22nd Wisconsin had been commanded to march straight into it.

William Utley had orders of his own to give. "Fix **bayonets**!" he shouted. Row after row of soldiers fitted their muskets with sharp bayonets and lined up in marching **formation**. Guns were loaded. Bayonets bristled like porcupine quills as more than 1,000 soldiers marched into Louisville. Fugitive slaves were armed with pistols. And they were marching in the center of the regiment.

"I hope there will be no **forcible** attempt to take [any]one," Reverend Bradley said. "If there is, *there will be music*." What music? The "music" of war—drumbeats of gunfire and the cymbal-clashing of bayonets! The 22nd Wisconsin would not surrender a single fugitive without a fight.

At the sight of the bayonets, the crowd pulled back. Would that Yankee colonel really fight for runaway slaves? Would the Wisconsin soldiers really use those bayonets?

---

bayonet: a long knife that can be fastened to the end of a rifle
formation: arranged in a particular way
forcible: using violence to make someone do something, especially against his or her will

As the troops approached, one slave catcher made a grab at a fugitive. A pistol fired. Reverend Bradley wrote what happened. "Snap went a cap! Fortunate for Mr. Slave Catcher that the pistol in the hands of the fugitive missed fire." Then the Kentucky men learned the 22nd Wisconsin would, indeed, use those bayonets. "A dozen bayonets **converged** to the spot where the slave hunter stood. Some evidently **penetrated** his clothes," Bradley wrote. That slave catcher could not get to the side of the street fast enough!

The Abolition Regiment kept marching. The crowd kept threatening and yelling. Guns and bayonets remained fixed and ready. In the end, the entire 22nd Wisconsin—soldiers *and* fugitives—marched on board a boat headed down the river.

What happened to the people in this story? The young woman rescued by Sergeant Berch and Corporal Rockwell arrived safely in Racine. She later married a young barber and set up housekeeping in Chicago.

Sergeant Berch became **quartermaster** for the 22nd Wisconsin. A few months after the troops left Louisville, Corporal Rockwell was badly wounded and sent home. Colonel William Utley was **sued** by one Kentucky slave owner for slave stealing.

One year later, the story of the 22nd Wisconsin was telegraphed across the entire Union by a New York newspaper reporter. "Surely, you brave men, who stood so firm at that time, as you read these pages, will rejoice," the report read. "You did well. The slave is now free."

---

converged: came together and formed a single unit
penetrated: went inside or through something
quartermaster: an army officer who provides clothing and food for a body of troops
sued: accused by someone in a court of law

11

LOOKING DOWN THE TRACK

From the earliest days of slavery in the United States, black people freed themselves. A few slaves won freedom by fighting in the Revolutionary War. Later, some worked extra jobs. They saved for years to buy themselves from their owners. Still others earned their freedom with their feet—they ran away.

Many stories tell how slaves ran north, toward Canada. Actually, people running from slavery headed in every direction. Some fled west. Some of them became pioneers or found safety with American Indian tribes.

No one knows how many fugitive slaves ran south to Mexico or to island countries like Cuba or Haiti. No one knows how many spent their lives hidden in the swamps and bayous of Florida and Louisiana.

A few enslaved people returned to their homelands in Africa. Some were helped by abolitionists who believed God had never intended black people to leave Africa. These abolitionists thought the only way to undo the crime of slavery was to send all black people to their rightful "home."

Some African Americans agreed. Some just wanted to leave the United States and the pain of slavery behind. They dreamed of building a free nation in Africa where every enslaved person could make a new life. Many more disagreed. They had never lived in Africa and considered themselves Americans. They wanted to live in this country as free citizens.

History also tells us that some proslavery people tried to force free blacks to "return" to Africa. Slave owners wanted the government to make free people leave their homes, jobs, and family members still trapped in slavery. These proslavery people thought if free black people were sent away, the slaves left behind would be easier to control.

No one knows how many people gained their freedom by running. No one knows, either, how many were caught and returned to slavery, or how many tried to flee and died in the attempt.

Freedom workers were found even in the far South, hundreds of miles from the nearest free state. Stories are told of Quakers and others who forged **passes**, hid runaways, and told slaves how to reach the free North. Some abolitionists traveled south just to free slaves. Some free black people and former slaves, like **Harriet Tubman**, risked their freedom and their lives to rescue others.

Harriet Tubman

Courtesy of Library of Congress, LC-USZ62-7816

---

pass: a signed paper showing the slave owner's permission for a slave to travel
Harriet Tubman: an abolitionist who was born a slave; she led many slaves to freedom on the
   Underground Railroad

Freedom Train North

The main routes on the Underground Railroad ran through Michigan, Illinois, Indiana, New York, Ohio, and Pennsylvania. Wisconsin was a "branch line" on this railroad to freedom—a back-road track used by small "trains" and few passengers. Wisconsin's freedom workers needed as much courage as those on the more-traveled routes of the Underground Railroad, however. Here, small groups of trusted and trusting friends relied on each other to help runaways reach the Great Lakes and Canada-bound freedom ships. When money was needed, the same people contributed again and again. The number of stations and workers was small, so every hand and hiding place was needed.

Wisconsin's freedom workers may not have been many in number, but they were strong and determined. When arrest warrants and jail doors stood in their way, they knocked them down—sometimes literally! When slave hunters came sniffing around like bloodhounds, abolitionists found creative ways to outwit them. Attics and cellars were not the only stations; a sugar barrel, a tunnel, and a warehouse on the Lake Michigan shore became part of the silent, secret work of our Underground Railroad. Free black people and former runaways in cities like Milwaukee and Racine or farm settlements like Pleasant Ridge helped former slaves find work and a safe place to stay.

Wisconsin's Underground Railroad must not be forgotten. These stories of people with courage to stand for freedom have lessons for us today.

Remember Lyman Goodnow's words about Waukesha's freedom workers? "We were very radical in our views of right and wrong. We opposed bad men everywhere; supported all fugitive slaves who came to us, and worked like beavers for the right."

Remember Dr. Dyer, an abolitionist from Burlington, Wisconsin, who said, "Can liberty and slavery long dwell together? Which side shall we be on? Surely we will be for liberty."

Even in Wisconsin, a free state, people had to choose between right and wrong. They had to take a stand for or against slavery. Every person who stood against slavery took a risk. Friends or neighbors might become enemies. Customers might take their business elsewhere. Everyone who helped fugitive slaves risked 6 months in jail and a $1,000 fine—3 years' wages! Still, when the question was asked, "Can you help?" person after person said, "Yes."

WHi Image ID 73952

Frederick Douglass was another escaped slave who worked hard to bring more slaves to freedom and to win more northerners to the cause of abolition.

African Americans and American Indians took the greatest risks of all. Indian tribes were already being pushed from their land onto reservations. By aiding escaped slaves, they risked more trouble with the government. Free black people and former slaves risked their freedom and their lives each time they helped a fugitive slave.

Fugitive slaves and freedom workers believed in every person's right to life and freedom. Even today, even in the United States, those rights are not always safe. People must still ask, "Which side shall we be on?" If Wisconsin's freedom workers could speak, they would tell us to follow the tracks of the Underground Railroad. They would say, "Be for liberty."

GLOSSARY

Pronunciation Key

a c<u>a</u>t (kat), pl<u>ai</u>d (plad), h<u>al</u>f (haf)

ah f<u>a</u>ther (**fah** THur), h<u>ea</u>rt (hahrt)

air c<u>a</u>rry (**kair** ee), b<u>ea</u>r (bair), wh<u>e</u>re (whair)

aw <u>a</u>ll (awl), l<u>aw</u> (law), b<u>ough</u>t (bawt)

ay s<u>ay</u> (say), br<u>ea</u>k (brayk), v<u>ei</u>n (vayn)

e b<u>e</u>t (bet), s<u>ay</u>s (sez), d<u>ea</u>f (def)

ee b<u>ee</u> (bee), t<u>ea</u>m (teem), f<u>ea</u>r (feer)

i b<u>i</u>t (bit), w<u>o</u>men (**wim** uhn), b<u>ui</u>ld (bild)

ı <u>i</u>ce (ıs), l<u>ie</u> (lı), sk<u>y</u> (skı)

o h<u>o</u>t (hot), w<u>a</u>tch (wotch)

oh <u>o</u>pen (**oh** puhn), s<u>ew</u> (soh)

oi b<u>oi</u>l (boil), b<u>oy</u> (boi)

oo p<u>oo</u>l (pool), m<u>o</u>ve (moov), sh<u>oe</u> (shoo)

or <u>or</u>der (**or** dur), m<u>or</u>e (mor)

ou h<u>ou</u>se (hous), n<u>ow</u> (nou)

u g<u>oo</u>d (gud), sh<u>ou</u>ld (shud)

uh c<u>u</u>p (kuhp), fl<u>oo</u>d (fluhd), b<u>utto</u>n (**buht** uhn)

ur b<u>ur</u>n (burn), p<u>ear</u>l (purl), b<u>ir</u>d (burd)

yoo <u>u</u>se (yooz), f<u>ew</u> (fyoo), v<u>iew</u> (vyoo)

hw <u>wh</u>at (hwuht), <u>wh</u>en (hwen)

th <u>th</u>at (THat), brea<u>the</u> (breeTH)

zh mea<u>s</u>ure (**mezh** ur), gara<u>g</u>e (guh **razh**)

abolitionist (ab uh **lish** uh nist): a person who is against slavery

accurate: exactly correct

ancestor: member of a family who lived a long time ago

ankle irons: iron cuffs worn around the ankle to prevent a slave from escaping

annual: happening once every year

antislavery: against slavery

appointed: chosen

archaeologist (ar kee **ol** uh jist): a scientist who learns about past people by studying objects left behind at places whcre people lived, worked, and played

Asahel (**a** suh hel)

assault (uh **sawlt**): to attack someone or something violently

barred: blocked to keep someone out

bayonet: a long knife that can be fastened to the end of a rifle

belfry (**bel** free): the tower, or room in a tower, where a large bell is hung

betray: turn against someone, especially in a time of need

betrayer: a person who turns against another

biracial (bɪ **ray** shuhl): part one race and part another

blood brother: a person who has sworn to treat another as his brother

bloodhound: a large dog with a wrinkled face, drooping ears, and a very good sense of smell

bondage (**bon** dij): slavery

border state: one of the slave states of Delaware, Maryland, Virginia, Kentucky, and Missouri that were next to the free states of the North during the Civil War

bounty hunter: a person who caught runaway slaves for money

bridle: straps that fit around a horse's head and mouth and are used to control it

brigadier general: an officer in the U.S. Army, Air Force, or Marine Corps ranking above colonel and below major general

John Brown: an American abolitionist who worked hard and fought with weapons against slavery

chaplain: a priest, minister, or rabbi who works in the military

chief justice: the head of the state's or country's court system

Civil War: the U.S. war between the southern states, or Confederacy, and the northern states, or Union, that lasted from 1861 to 1865

claim shanty: a rough hut or cabin, built to claim a piece of land

colonel (**kur** nuhl): an officer in the U.S. Army, Air Force, or Marine Corps ranking below a general

compromise (**kom** pruh mɪz): to agree to accept something that is not exactly what you wanted

Confederate (kuhn **fed** ur uht): having to do with the South during the Civil War

content: happy and satisfied

contraband (**kon** truh band): goods brought illegally from one place to another

contrary: opposite

converged: came together and formed a single unit

Daugherty (**doh** uhr tee)

dawdling: doing something slowly, wasting time

defied (di **fīd**): refused to obey

desperately (**des** puh ruht lee): in immediate need of help

disguise: something that hides a person's identity

distorted: changed or twisted

dockhand: someone who works where ships load and unload cargo

documented: recorded with factual support

drilled: did something over and over again in order to learn it well

drought (drout): a long spell of very dry weather

Emancipation Proclamation (i man si **pay** shun prok luh **may** shun): a document signed by Abraham Lincoln in 1863 declaring the slaves free

enforce: to make sure a rule or law is obeyed

escorting: accompanying someone, especially for protection

evidence: information and facts that help prove something is true

exhibit: a display at a museum

fair-weather: loyal only during a time of success

flailed: moved, swung, or beat

forcible: using violence to make someone do something, especially against his or her will

formation: arranged in a particular way

freedman: a person who had been a slave and who bought, was given, or took his or her freedom

fugitive (**fyoo** juh tiv): someone who is running away, especially from the police

generation: all the people born around the same time

grieve: to feel very sad because someone has died

griot (**gree** oh)

hawked: offered goods for sale by shouting in the street

hoisted: lifted something heavy

homesteader: someone who has been given land to settle on and work by the U.S. government

landmark: an important building or place

legally: according to the law

legislature (**lej** uh slay chur): an elected group of people who have the power to make or change laws for a city, state, or nation

loyalty: support or faithfulness to one's country, family, friends, or beliefs

manure: animal waste put on land to help crops grow better

memoir (**mem** wahr): a true story written about a person's own life

migrated: to move from one country or region to another

miniature (**min** ee uh chur): smaller than the usual size

missionary (**mish** shuh nair ee): someone who is sent by a church or religious group to teach a group's faith

modest: not boastful

Mohican (moh **hee** kuhn)

noble-hearted: idealistic, considerate

obedient (oh **bee** dee uhnt): doing what one is told to do

obliged: expected to do something

oral history: history that is spoken, not written

orphaned: without any parents

pardoned: forgave or excused from punishment

Freedom Train North

parlor: a formal living room used for receiving guests

parsonage: the house provided by a church for its pastor

pass: a signed paper showing the slave owner's permission for a slave to travel

pastor: a minister or priest in charge of a church

penetrated: went inside or through something

politician (pol uh **tish** uhn): someone who runs for or holds a government office, such as a senator

prairie: a large area of flat or rolling grassland with few or no trees

precious (**presh** uhs): very special or dear

professional: a member of a profession, such as teacher, doctor, nurse, or lawyer

proslavery: in favor of slavery

pursuer: a person chasing someone or something

Quaker: a member of the Society of Friends, a Christian group that opposes war and prefers simple religious services

quartermaster: an army officer who provides clothing and food for a body of troops

radical (**ra** di kuhl): extreme

rebellion: armed fight against the government

refuge: protection or shelter

refugee: someone who is forced to leave his or her home because of war, persecution, or natural disaster

regiment: a military unit made up of 500 to 1,000 soldiers

register: a book in which names or official records are kept

reputation (rep yoo **tay** shuhn): a person's worth or character, as judged by other people

reservation: federal land reserved or set aside for Indian nations to live on

reverend: title used for a minister or other clergy

sacrificed: given up for a reason

satchel: a bag or small suitcase

scare-up: a trip to get something or finish something that is hard to do

scrounged: collected things with difficulty

sergeant (**sahr** juhnt): an officer in the U.S. Army or Air Force who is second in command of a small group of soldiers

shanty: roughly built hut or cabin, often made of wood

Sharps rifle: a weapon common in the Civil War era

shawl: a piece of soft material worn over the shoulders or around the head

shuttling: regularly traveling back and forth along the same route

smuggle: bring goods or people into a place illegally

sprinted: ran fast for a short distance

staggered: walked unsteadily

Stars and Stripes: the flag of the United States

sued: accused by someone in a court of law

supreme court: the most powerful court in a state or country

survived: stayed alive through a dangerous event

telegraphed: sent a message using a code of electrical signals sent by wire or radio

territorial (ter uh **tor** ee uhl): having to do with a particular land or region

territory: a part of the U.S. not yet admitted as a state

testify: to state the truth or give evidence in court

transformed: greatly changed

trench: a long, narrow ditch used to protect soldiers in battle

Harriet Tubman: an abolitionist who was born a slave; she led many slaves to freedom on the Underground Railroad

Union Army: the military that fought for the northern states during the Civil War

unjust: not fair or right

veteran: someone who has served in the armed forces

widower: a man whose wife has died

Yankee: someone born or living in the northern states

TO LEARN MORE

If you want to learn more about the stories in *Freedom Train North*, the following sources will be useful. All books can be obtained through your public library via interlibrary loan. Full bibliographic information can be found in the bibliography.

Introduction: History, Legend, and Story

To learn more about oral history, try *My Backyard History Book* by David Weitzman, Little, Brown Publishers, or *Celebrating Everyday Life in Wisconsin History* by Dr. Bobbie Malone of the Wisconsin Historical Society Press.

Chapter 1: Freedom Dreams

The Refugee: Narratives of Fugitive Slaves in Canada by Benjamin Drew is an entire book of stories told by people like William Hall who freed themselves from slavery by running.

Chapter 2: Independence Day

Caroline Quarlls's story was told best by her friend Lyman Goodnow in the Western Historical Company book *The History of Waukesha County*. A short version is also in *The Underground Railroad* by Charles Blockson. I tell the whole story in my book *Caroline Quarlls and the Underground Railroad*, published by the Wisconsin Historical Society Press.

Note: If you research Caroline's life by reading some of these books, you may find her last name spelled in different ways. For example, Lyman Goodnow spelled it Quarles. Caroline's descendants in Canada believe it was spelled Quarlls, so that spelling was used in this book.

Chapter 3: Strong against Slavery

The Underground Railroad by Charles Blockson and *Reminiscences of Levi Coffin* by Levi Coffin discuss who participated in the Underground Railroad and why.

The best source for Wisconsin's Underground Railroad history is *Negro Slavery in Wisconsin and the Underground Railroad* by John Nelson Davidson. A copy of this pamphlet can be requested through interlibrary loan. Your librarian will find it in the Dane County (Wisconsin) System Collection.

Chapter 4: Jailbreak!

Read about Joshua Glover's story in the Western Historical Company book *The History of Milwaukee, Wisconsin, Volume II.*

Chapter 5: Secret Service

The whole story of the Porters and the family of fugitives is told in *Eliza Chappell Porter: A Memoir* by Mary Porter, or in Davidson's *Negro Slavery in Wisconsin and the Underground Railroad*, both available through interlibrary loan. The Milton Historical Society website mentioned under Chapter 6 includes Eliza's own words about their experiences helping people running from slavery.

Chapter 6: Overground, Underground

Go online to find out more about the Milton House and Hiram and Eliza Foote in Janesville. At www.miltonhouse.org you can also learn about Eliza and Jeremiah Porter, Joshua Glover, and Caroline Quarlls, about routes and stops on the Underground Railroad, and about how Milton House became Wisconsin's National Underground Railroad Landmark.

Chapter 7: Sketches from the Road

Some stories in this chapter are included in Davidson's *Negro Slavery in Wisconsin and the Underground Railroad*. To find out more about the Underground Railroad in any of the towns mentioned in this chapter you'll have to write or visit the town or historical society. Ask your librarian or the Wisconsin Historical Society for addresses of local societies.

Chapter 8: Open the Window and Jump!

Jacob Green ran from slavery 4 times before he finally reached freedom. He tells the whole story in *Narrative of the Life of J. D. Green, a Runaway Slave, from Kentucky*. Your librarian can obtain a copy through interlibrary loan from the Dane County Library System. You can even see the original antislavery pamphlet where Jacob Green's story was first printed. Go to the Library of Congress website at http://lcweb2.loc.gov/cgi-bin/query/r?ammem/AMALL:@field%28DOCID+@ lit%2891899129%29%29. Click on "view page images" and "view text" to see for yourself!

Chapter 9: Open Hearts, Open Hands

More information is available in the book *War Pictures: Experiences and Observations of a Chaplain* by Reverend James Rogers.

Chapter 10: Soldier Heroes of the Underground Railroad

The story of Colonel Utley and the brave 22nd Wisconsin is told in *The Star Corps* by Reverend George Bradley, *War Pictures* by Reverend James Rogers, and *Reminiscences of Levi Coffin* by Levi Coffin. In *The Underground Railroad*, Charles Blockson tells the young girl's story.

◆　◆　◆　◆

These books and other materials are recommended for further study of the Underground Railroad in the United States.

Young Readers

Many Thousand Gone: African Americans from Slavery to Freedom by Virginia Hamilton. Knopf, New York, 2002.

Tales from the Underground Railroad by Kate Connell. Raintree, Metropolitan Teaching & Learning, Frederick, Colorado, 1993.

The Underground Railroad by Raymond Bial. Houghton Mifflin, Chicago, 2000.

Older Readers

Get on Board: The Story of the Underground Railroad by James Haskins. Scholastic, New York, 1995.

Bound for the North Star: True Stories of Fugitive Slaves by Dennis Brindell Fradin. Clarion Books/Houghton Mifflin Harcourt, New York, 2000.

Fleeing to Freedom on the Underground Railroad: The Courageous Slaves, Agents, and Conductors by Elaine Landau. Twenty-First Century Books/Lerner Publishing Group, Minneapolis, 2006.

Incidents in the Life of a Slave Girl by Harriet Jacobs. Mariner Books/Houghton Mifflin Harcourt Trade and Reference, New York, 2010.

To Be a Slave by Julius Lester. Puffin/Penguin, New York, 2005.

Other Resources

Cricket Magazine. February 1995 issue.

National Geographic Magazine. July 1984 and September 1992.

Try searching these addresses on the Internet:
   http://www.ugrr.org/ugrr
   http://www.miltonhouse.org
   http://www.loc.gov/ammem/ (slave narratives, Library of Congress American Memories Collection)

The Underground Railroad: Songs and Stories of Freedom by Kim and Reggie Harris. Chatham Hill Games, Phone: 800-554-3039. CD, audiotape, and video on UGRR history. Boardgame.

BIBLIOGRAPHY

This list includes all sources used to write *Freedom Train North*. When a source provided information for a specific chapter, those chapter numbers are listed. Some sources provided general information about the Underground Railroad. Primary sources (firsthand descriptions of events by people who witnessed them or participated) are noted by an asterisk (*).

Books and Journals

American Memory. Washington D.C.: Library of Congress African American Pamphlet Collection; Daniel Murray Collection, 1820–1920.

Blockson, Charles. *The Underground Railroad.* New York: Prentice-Hall, 1987. (Chapters 2, 10.)

Bradley, G[eorge] S. *The Star Corps; or Notes of an Army Chaplain, During Sherman's Famous "March to the Sea."* Milwaukee: Jermain and Brightman, Book and Job Printers, 1865. (Chapter 10.)*

Coffin, Levi. *Reminiscences of Levi Coffin: The Reputed President of the Underground Railroad.* Cincinnati: Robert Clarke, 1880. (Chapters 9, 10.)*

Davidson, John Nelson. *Negro Slavery in Wisconsin and the Underground Railroad.* Milwaukee: Parkman Club Publications, No. 18, September 14, 1897. (Chapters 1, 2, 4, 5, 7.)*

Drew, Benjamin. *The Refugee: Narratives of Fugitive Slaves in Canada*. Boston: John P. Jewett and Company, 1856. (Chapter 1.)*

Finch, Asahel. *Milwaukee Bar Association Meeting Records upon the death of General James H. Paine*. Milwaukee: Milwaukee Bar Association, 1879.*

Foote, Eliza. *The 50th Anniversary of the First Congregational Church, Janesville, Wis.* Janesville, Wisconsin: First Congregational Church, 1895. (Chapter 6.)*

The Fugitive Slave Law and Its Victims, Anti-Slavery Tracts, No. 15. New York: American Anti-Slavery Society, 1861.

Green, Jacob. *Narrative of the Life of J. D. Green, a Runaway Slave, from Kentucky*. Huddersfield, Canada: Henry Fielding, Pack Horse Yard, 1864. (Chapter 8.)*

Haviland, Laura S. *A Woman's Life-work: Labors and Experiences*. Cincinnati: Walden and Stowe, 1881. (Chapter 9.)*

Henson, Josiah. *The Life of Josiah Henson . . . As Narrated by Himself.* Boston: Arthur D. Phelps, 1849.*

Hill, Daniel G. *The Freedom Seekers: Blacks in Early Canada*. Agincourt, Canada: Book Society of Canada, 1981.

The Home Missionary, Vol. 66, No. 7. Chicago: Home Mission Society (Methodist), 1893. (Chapter 5.)

Howe, Samuel Gridley. *The Refugees from Slavery in Canada West: Report to the Freedman's Commission*. Boston: Wright and Potter, 1864.*

Kartak, Mollie Maurer. "Memories of My Childhood," *Wisconsin Magazine of History*, Vol. 10, No. 4. Madison: State Historical Society of Wisconsin, 1927. (Chapter 7.)*

Leach, Eugene W. *The Racine County Militant*. Racine, Wisconsin: E. W. Leach, 1915. (Chapters 8, 10.)

Mathews, Edward. *The Autobiography of the Rev[erend] E[dward] Mathews*. New York: American Baptist Free Mission Society, 1866. (Chapters 2, 3, 5.)*

Noonan, Barry. *Blacks in Canada: 1861, Lists and Analysis*. Madison: State Historical Society of Wisconsin, 1997. (Chapters 2, 4.)

Olin, Chauncey C. *A Complete Record of the John Olin Family*. Indianapolis: Baker-Randolph, 1893. (Chapters 2, 4.)

Petit, Eber M. *Sketches in the History of the Underground Railroad*. Fredonia, New York: McKinstry and Sons, 1879.*

Pond, J. B. *Eccentrics of Genius*. New York: W. Dillingham, 1900. (Chapter 7.)*

Porter, Mary A. *Eliza Chappell Porter: A Memoir*. Chicago: Fleming Revell, 1880. (Chapter 5.)*

Rogers, James B. *War Pictures: Experiences and Observations of a Chaplain in the U.S. Army in the War of the Southern Rebellion*. Chicago: Church and Goodman, 1863. (Chapters 9, 10.)*

The Sabbath Recorder. Janesville, Wisconsin: Seventh Day Baptist Church, 1854. (Chapter 6.)

Ward, Samuel Ringgold. *Autobiography of a Fugitive Negro*. London, 1855. Reprint, Chicago: Johnson, 1970.*

Regional Histories

Current, Richard. *The History of Wisconsin, Volume II, 1848–1873*. Madison: State Historical Society of Wisconsin, 1976. (Chapters 4, 5.)

The History of Milwaukee, Wisconsin, Volume II. Chicago: Western Historical Company, 1881. (Chapters 2, 3, 4.)

A History of Racine and Kenosha Counties. Chicago: Western Historical Company, 1879. (Chapters 2, 4.)

The History of the Burlington Plymouth Congregational Church. Burlington, Wisconsin: Burlington Plymouth Congregational Church, 1908. (Chapter 7.)

The History of Walworth County, Wisconsin. Chicago: Western Historical Company, 1882. (Chapter 2, 3.)

The History of Waukesha County. Chicago: Western Historical Company, 1880. (Chapters 2, 3.)

Jensen, Don. *Kenosha Kaleidoscope: Images of the Past*. Kenosha, Wisconsin: Kenosha Historical Society, 1985. (Chapter 7.)

Lyman, Frank. *The City of Kenosha and Kenosha County, Wisconsin*. Chicago: J. S. Clarke, 1916. (Chapter 7.)

Newspapers

Advocate. March 1854–December 1860. Text-fiche, State Historical Society of Wisconsin, Madison. (Chapter 4.)

Aegis. March 2, 1841. Text-fiche, State Historical Society of Wisconsin, Madison.

Milwaukee Daily Sentinel. March 1854–December 1860. Milwaukee. Text-fiche, State Historical Society of Wisconsin, Madison. (Chapter 7.)*

Wisconsin Free Democrat. September 16, 1850–February 20, 1860. Milwaukee and Waukesha, Wisconsin. Text-fiche, State Historical Society of Wisconsin, Madison. (Chapter 4.) Contains some primary source material related to Glover rescue and Booth case.

Manuscript Sources

Dutton, Achas P. Papers. Racine, Wisconsin: Racine Heritage Museum, 1901. (Chapter 8.)*

Goodrich Family Papers. Milton, Wisconsin: Manuscripts Collections, Milton Historical Society, undated. (Chapter 6.)*

Landon, Frederick. Fred Landon Papers, unbound. Canada: J. J. Talman Regional Collection, D. B. Weldon Library, University of Western Ontario. Text-fiche copy available as Fred Landon Papers.

"Memoirs of Captain Theodore Fellows," *Manuscripts in Old and New, Vol. IV.* Kenosha, Wisconsin: Kenosha Historical Society, undated.

Olin, Chauncey C. "A History of the Early Anti-slavery Excitement in the State of Wisconsin." Manuscript Collection, Western Reserve Historical Society, Cleveland, Ohio. Text-fiche copy, State Historical Society of Wisconsin, Madison. (Chapters 2, 4.)*

Siebert, Wilbur H. *The Underground Railroad in Wisconsin.* Ohio State University, Columbus, Ohio, 1893. Copy in Rare Books Collection, State Historical Society of Wisconsin, Madison. (Chapters 1, 3, 8.)*

Underwood Family Papers. Wauwatosa, Wisconsin: Collections, Underwood Baptist Church, undated. (Chapter 3.)*

ACKNOWLEDGMENTS

Freedom Train North was first published by Living History Press in 1998. Many people helped make this book possible. Among them are Jack Holzhueter, Pleasant Rowland, librarians and archivists at the Wisconsin Historical Society, and the wonderful people at the Milton Historical Society.

Special thanks to Maureen McGilligan-Bentin, Dave Messman, Kate Fitzgerald-Fleck, and many other teachers and librarians who have helped bring these stories to life by inviting me to present storytelling programs in their classrooms, creating amazing curricula, and using this book as a resource to teach children about integrity, justice, and the courage to do what is right.

Thanks to Dr. Phyllis Tousey Fredericks, Ms. Loretta Metoxen, and Ms. Shelia Powless for sharing information about Wisconsin American Indian history.

The author salutes so many librarians, including Julie Chase of the Dane County Library system and the staff of Middleton Library, for invaluable assistance.

Thank you to the Waukesha family whose generosity kept the Quarlls letters from being lost to history.

Finally, the author is deeply grateful to and for Mrs. Charlotte Watkins, great-great-granddaughter of Caroline Quarlls Watkins, who treated the author like a daughter. Bless you, Charlotte.

INDEX

This index points you to the pages where you can read about persons, places, and ideas. If you do not find the word you are looking for, try to think of another word that means about the same thing.

When you see a page number in **bold** it means there is a picture on that page.

ABOUT THE AUTHOR

Julia Pferdehirt is an author, educator, and professional storyteller. A resident of Middleton, Wisconsin, Pferdehirt is also the author of *They Came to Wisconsin*, *Caroline Quarlls and the Underground Railroad*, and *Blue Jenkins: Working for Workers*, all published for young audiences by the Wisconsin Historical Society Press.